A Voice

in the

Dark

By: Patty Sabatier

An alternative to medication alone for the treatment of mental illness

A Voice in the Dark

An alternative to medication alone for the treatment of mental illness.

A Personal Story of Triumph Over Bipolar Mental Illness

This book is non-fiction and as such is meant to share a journey of one woman, the author. It is not meant to be a guideline for treatment of all mental disorders. It is imperative that a reader who chooses to begin a Jungian spirituality for treatment of mental illness do so with the help of a Jungian therapist and specifically not alone.

Printed in the United States of America

by CreateSpace. Copies are available through CreateSpace.com or by

contacting the author.

Cover design and art by Patty Sabatier

Graphics by Betty Berk-Gong

ISBN:13-978-1492844716

About the Author

Patty Sabatier is a native of Louisiana, who as a Navy nurse and Catholic Nun, struggled with undiagnosed bipolar mental illness. Diagnosed at age 28, she began a long heroic journey with this darkness. With the aid of Jungian spirituality and psychotherapy, she was able to integrate all the difficult episodes of her 65 years of life. She presently lives in California, with her husband, Ron, and is a Public Health Nurse. Patty dedicates this book to all her relatives in this generation and in the future generations. Patty can be reached by readers at pattysabatier@gmail.com. She welcomes comments and questions regarding this book.

How beautiful on the Mountains

How beautiful on the mountains
Are the feet of one who brings good news
Feet that have been bruised and torn
But kept on walking
Bare upon the groaning earth
Without the comfort shoes afford.

Harder than walking over seas
You walk with us.

My heart shakes off
Her dull and withered leaves
Becomes a burning bush
Before your feet.

By Heidi Neumark
1977
Reprinted with permission of the author

Acknowledgements

In this book, I focus on only those events that contributed to my struggle with mental illness. There were many experiences of joy, playfulness and celebration in my childhood and all through my adult years. These experiences served to keep me afloat through the dark periods. But in this book, I focus predominately on the dark periods. I apologize to all those who loved me and expressed that love every day. I realize you must have felt helpless in trying to enable me to find wholeness and happiness. I feel no person is responsible for my dark journey. It is the road I was born to walk. I want to say thank you to my parents, brothers and sisters, Navy friends, the Catholic Nuns and my first husband's family. You all contributed to my victory over mental illness with your persistent openness to me.

I also want to thank the Visalia Writer's Group from Visalia, California and Peter Reed, who critiqued my writing over several years and helped me bring this book to life. They enabled me to clarify and verbalize a mysterious, complex life story. In particular, I want to thank Betty Berk-Gong and Dr. Avak Howsepian whose consistent encouragement and belief in my story enabled me to persist through the labor and delivery of this book. Without them, it may not have come to be published. Betty Berk-Gong and Gloria Getman were also very helpful with the graphics for the publication.

I want to make a comment about my formal diagnosis of **bipolar mental illness**. My particular disease manifestation involved psychotic features, such as paranoia and hallucinations. Not all people with this diagnosis have these tendencies. Perhaps because my illness was caused by biochemical and environmental factors, I had these added features. I also want the reader to know that no matter how much counseling and art was involved, I never stopped my medications. I accepted that there was something chemically wrong with me and that I needed the meds. I think this added to my healing journey. I have known many mentally ill people whom, when they feel better, stop their meds and subsequently experience a resurgence of their disease. There are many new medications with fewer side effects available to treat this disease. Throughout my book, I emphasize the power of therapy and art to heal, but I also believe that medications are essential for this healing process.

Contents

Preface

Have you ever been so anxious, afraid, or confused that you could not make a choice or discern an action? Has life ever overwhelmed you so much that you gave up dealing with it and buried all your struggles in denial? Have your hopes and dreams for the future ever slammed directly into conflict with your memories and wounds from the past?

This is how I would describe my experience with a psychotic break and mental illness. The road out of the darkness these questions suggest can be long and arduous. This book is about that long difficult road to healing of mental illness.

"Mental illness accounts for more disability in developed countries than any other group of illnesses, including cancer and heart disease." (MMWR, September 2, 2011). In a family of four, according to the Center for Disease Control, one of you likely has a mental illness. Yet, even these staggering statistics do not compel the media to present more about how to prevent, recognize or treat these disorders.

My story is directly aimed at helping others heal through the creative arts and Jungian spirituality. This book is the story of my life journey. It is organized into three parts: my childhood and college years, my young adult years and my mid-life years. It is presented with my memories that relate best to my journey with mental illness. Names of family and friends have been changed to provide privacy. There are reflections following the memories, relating them to my present day thoughts. As you read, I hope you will find gold nuggets you can use to enrich and heal your own life journey.

I hope to weave a ribbon of three threads that wind and whirl all through my life: one red thread is the relationships that have always connected me to life, second is the black thread of mental illness and its dark challenge to my existence, and finally the white thread of my Jungian spirituality and its call to creativity.

This multicolored three-threaded ribbon connected me like an umbilical cord to the origin and source of my life, and today allows me to fulfill my destiny. This ribbon I lovingly extend to others who are drowning in the dark energies of mental illness. May you clasp it solidly and find your own creative way to express the sacred journey you have been chosen to walk.

My vision of mental illness is that it is only for the courageous and gifted ones in our society who are sensitive enough to walk where the majority will venture only when a safe, well-trodden path has been developed. I feel as though I have walked most of my life alone in a dark forest where psychic energies have overwhelmed the task of living. It was only art and Jungian spirituality that allowed these overpowering complexities from my unconscious to find a place of appropriate expression in my daily life. It is my hope that the telling of my journey will enable you to walk your path a little easier and closer to the origin and destiny of your call.

Hopefully, this story will help the friends and families of those who are marked with a journey through mental illness. I hope my journey will help these friends and families to celebrate the gift of their loved ones who are called to uniqueness in our society.

Due to the complexity of my story and Jungian spirituality, I have created a glossary at the end of the book. Words typed in bold are defined in this glossary for your reference. Also, at the end of the book are a series of meditations meant to share with you the spiritual nature of my healing journey.

A Voice in the Dark: Overview

Born into a family of doctors, nurses, engineers, and a physicist, I have known all my life of the wall that exists between scientific study and the creative arts. With a bachelor's degree in nursing, I also worshipped reality that could be tested and proven valid with scientific reasoning and research. But deep within was the artist who is captivated by the inexplicable mystery and the spiritual dimension of life, suffering and healing.

How this healing takes place through the arts is perhaps the most mysterious scientific fact research has not yet validated. But it is a fact of life; I know from firsthand experience.

When I was twenty-eight years old, I was overcome with the stresses of early adulthood and experienced a psychotic break, marked by incoherence and distorted perceptions of reality. This episode left me confused and frightened of God and myself. In this madness, I knew the light of insightful reasoning as too bright to bear, and squinting my eyes was the only way to see and endure the pain of this intrusion. I frequently squinted my eyes, trying to see and make sense of what I thought, heard and saw. Stimuli from everything within and without were disorganized, poignant and pregnant with potential meaning and direction. Though everything in my outer world seemed to have messages for my inner world, I lacked the ego strength to discern and organize these messages into any meaningful action.

Opposing thoughts constantly pressured my awareness and wrecked my ability to choose even in the simplest matters. Fear of travel outside my home gripped me while voices taunted me to make decisions. Depression countered by racing thoughts and emotions kept me from any form of lasting success in life.

Thoughts of inflicting harm on others and myself overwhelmed my inner **soul** and mind. Washing my hands and doorknobs could not remove the germs and fingerprints that all pointed inward. Guilt, hope, despair and exuberant joy all in one moment of clarity were always shrouded with the omnipresence of the **Dark side of God**. Where does one turn for relief? Fear marks all encounters both in self and with others. I was a leper and a soothsayer, and found home only on the edges of society. Neither society nor myself could tolerate my message of guilt, death and truth organized in a chaotic, symbolic system of thought, expressed in paranoia.

I had never been exposed, prior to this event, to art and creativity from the soul as a source of healing and integration of opposites. My birth family and nursing education did not respect or encourage these energies. But desperate in my midlife years for a sense of inner integrity, identity, and my place in the world, I sought out Jungian therapy, and my own **individuation** through drawing, painting, sculpturing, creative writing and dream interpretation. Playing with symbols from my inner **psyche** for many years, I allowed the artist within to raise me up, heal old wounds, and shape a new vision for me.

In this creative struggle, all life began to flow through the single point of my pen in journal writing, with my controlling ego surrendered to the service of this emerging life. All light and insight serviced my eyes as they bore witness to the wisdom of beauty seen in everything. My hands learned to touch the canvas and the clay, leaving the presence of **Self** behind for the sake of truth. I died daily by letting go of fears, resentments, and failures. This peeling of layers enabled insight to emerge as a new expression of life found within the context of my artistic creations.

Madness serves its purpose as the chaos out of which creativity gleans its unlimited elements and develops its messages of beauty, truth and insight. Creativity is the embracing with precision, skill and love, the dark chaotic matter of madness.

Through this journey with mental illness, I grew in all my skills: as a nurse now in the field of HIV/AIDS care, as a wife, and as a friend to others. Today, I find within me the ability to move through life with ease and joy, something my young years did not allow. If my story is a source of hope and healing for others, it is only because the artist within me has created a space for these values to flourish, utilizing the many-colored palettes which suffering and experience bring to one's soul.

The theme of this book is primarily one of learning the appropriate balance between logic and feelings. I have spent a lifetime discovering how logic can critique and destroy valuable feelings. Within my soul, I have had to learn that masculine logic must be the servant of what one values and cherishes. The thinking masculine energy must serve, revere and refine the feminine. This honing energy should spring from love and compassion, not invasion, possession or violation.

As my story unfolds, you will see that I learned to isolate and tame the harsh masculine energy of logic, demanding within myself, that it accept the boundaries imposed by the needs of the feminine emotions which value relationships more than reasoning.

It is my hope that somehow this manuscript will be a starting point for many others to creatively embrace the madness that swells to overcome their conscious lives in times of stress, neurosis or psychosis. My particular story involved an inheritance of mental illness on both sides of my family histories. The environment in which I grew up also contributed to my struggles with sanity. Only through an appreciation of **Depth Psychology** was I able to make sense of these two worlds and their influences on my life. The environment of my childhood and the biochemical imbalance in my brain created the tensions of my life that determined who I was and who I was to become. It was essential that I come to grips with the two worlds of my heritage, the genealogical and the environmental.

Added to this heritage, was the uniqueness of my nature, the identity buried in my psyche, the star in my heart that would compel me to make a singular journey. I had to come to grips with a call of a wounded healer and its special demands in my life.

My story begins with my childhood. Born at the end of the 1940's, I grew up in the peaceful southern world of Jeff Davis Parish of Southwestern Louisiana. I knew of no one who went off to war during my childhood. World War II was over and the Korean conflict did not intersect with my personal world as a child. My father, Michael, was a large, handsome man with coal black hair. He stood exactly six feet tall and often jokingly bragged that there were only two people in the

7

world exactly six feet tall, himself and Jesus Christ. He served during World War II as a flight surgeon. He was thirty-three years old when his fourth child, second daughter, Patricia was born. His profession was a private practice physician and the Coroner for Jeff Davis Parish. When he retired at fifty-five, he began to work as an emergency room physician and an alcohol abuse physician with local agencies. He practiced medicine at a time when doctors delivered babies in their homes and families often paid him with farm produce. In general practice at that time, the physician's work often included general surgery that today is done only by specialists. He was a busy doctor in a rural area.

Gail, my mother, was a slender, 5'2" dark haired homemaker who grew up on a farm in Elton, Louisiana, part of near-by Allen Parish. She used to say she knew at age ten she would never marry a farmer because the life was filled with physical hardships. Regardless of this focus, she still told many stories of her adventures on the farm of playing in the haystacks of the barn and teasing the fenced-in bulls and cattle. Her father was a rice farmer, while Daddy's family was in the mercantile business. Mama and Daddy raised eight children with two miscarriages that they wished had also been born.

On a cold Christmas Eve, at age thirty-two, Mama brought from the hospital her fourth child to a home with no decorations for the season. It was a busy night for Michael as he was called out to the hospital in the middle of putting up the Christmas tree. Frustrated with the crooked tree and the demands of being a father and doctor, he quickly nailed the tree to the wall to stabilize it and rushed off to the hospital.

How Mama managed three other children all under the age of five and a newborn must have been difficult that evening.

Many years later, at age twenty, I felt drawn to join the Navy during the Vietnam War. It was not war that attracted me, nor patriotism that moved me. Somehow the poster inviting me to sign up for duty looked like a welcoming family that would be a bridge to my freedom. I felt trapped as the daughter of Michael and his aggressive handling of life. There was a philosophy for his approach to everything he did. It was engraved on a bronze plaque and given to him on his fiftieth birthday. It read, "If it jams, force it. If it breaks, it needed replacing anyway." This sentence explained his approach to everything from working on cars to raising children. As a family we laughed about this on his birthday, but deep inside it felt brutal and disrespectful to the delicate side of all life.

During my Navy years, I became enamored by the effective, gentle, nourishing approach to life I saw in the Catholic Nuns around my duty station in Virginia. These women were all well educated and had left traditional orders to found a new order more integrated into the society of the sixties and seventies. They were the Sisters For Christian Community. These nuns chose to take regular jobs, did not wear habits and sought to embrace with friendship people from all walks of life. My dad called them "hippy nuns." I called them "sacred women."

But even they could not hold me down to a committed life. Undiagnosed and poorly treated mental illness kept me from peacefully settling down anywhere in my twenties, thirties, or forties. I moved from Religious Life to my first marriage that also failed at age forty. There was a thread throughout my adult life that provided continuity for all my journeying. It was a deep desire to be healthy and whole mentally. I sought this mental wholeness through a Jungian approach to myself and life. Journal keeping, prayer and meditation were consistently the center of my wandering wheel. I will explain this approach to life as my book develops.

Jungian Spirituality and Depth Psychology.

For those of you who have no background in Jungian psychology, I want to give a brief foundation for reading this book. A full comprehension of Jungian psychology is beyond me, but I hope to explain those aspects that contributed to my healing. A lifetime of study could be done in this area of thought and not exhaust it. Please bear with me as I attempt to detail a very mysterious psychology. If you would prefer to begin with my story itself, you could move on to the next chapter and refer back to this chapter later when you need more understanding of certain principles and terminology.

In depth psychology, one is invited to appreciate facets of his or her own unconscious self. These facets are found by exploring and understanding one's nighttime dreams, fantasies and imagination. There are many images found there which all humans share. These are the building blocks of personality and are called **archetypes**. These original models of what it is to be human, such as father, mother, child, woman, man, daughter, son, sister, brother, hold tremendous energy for the expression of our unique selves.

Knowing and relating to the particular archetypes that are activated in your own unconscious world enables you to mature and become whole. Archetypes will affect our real life relationships in positive and negative ways. It is our responsibility to know how this happens and to channel that archetype's energy into a positive impact on our world. It is through this manner of self-discovery and expression that we come to individuation. Individuation is the unique development of our self and our life story. My book is a picture of my journey into individuation. That journey is still in process, but this book presents the major contributions that a Jungian approach gave to the healing of my bi-polar mental illness.

Carl Jung discovered for us the building blocks for the life of the soul and personality, both for the individual and the world soul, for society and the **collective unconscious**. These building blocks are called **archetypes.** They are identified as we search our dreams and imagination or the myths we hold dear. Some of the archetypes expressed in my dream world were found in the **myths** involving the **Minotaur, the wounded feminine, witch or madwoman**, and the **divine child**. I find that the myths involving these examples are found only in ancient stories and mythology no longer readily available to our present thinking. But those of you who have studied Greek Mythology and other ancient myths may be able to relate to these particular archetypes. Perhaps the story of **Persephone** comes to mind. The most commonly known story of the divine child is the birth of Christ. I will elaborate on theses archetypes later in my life story. I will refer to them in my book as they became identified in my life. Archetypes challenge us in the journey of becoming our unique self. They also enable us to answer who God is in our life and what our view of God demands from us.

The Jungian way is ultimately about searching for one's unique and gifted self. It is about searching for balance and wholeness in the personality, through involvement with the teachings of Carl Jung. It requires faithful attention to one's dreams, fantasies, imagination and daily life in order to find one's unique path. This way enabled me to discover why God created me. I discovered how God called me forth every day to an ultimate purpose of wholeness and integrity. Dealing with an inner identity as a wounded healer has taken a lifetime and is still unfolding.

As you discover the archetypes and myths that make up your own unconscious, you will discover a call from them to understand and work with them in a creative, constructive manner. This opens the way to a spiritual journey.

An example of an archetype and a spiritual journey is found in understanding the **Self.** The Self, an archetype identified by Jung, could be said to be the Divine expressing Itself from within our personality. The Self, as the center and controlling force of my whole personality, invites me to work with both my strengths and weaknesses. My view of the Self is that it is always unfolding and showing me more of itself with each dream I have. I am still seeking greater appreciation of the Self within me.

In order to be faithful to God, I must seek out a clear understanding of the Self as it unfolds and tells me what the Divine in me is all about. Dream work is the essential key to unlocking the mystery of God or the Self in me. The Self reveals and develops throughout my lifetime. This is the spiritual journey we are all called to make when seeking a Jungian view of life. I have come to view the Self as the unfolding of the evolutionary process of God's own journey with humankind. For me, Self and God are closely identified.

There are multitudes of spiritual pathways around today. These Christian and non-Christian lifestyles are all valid ways of journeying to God. Often, these sacred paths are based on a single person's journey with and experience of God. To my way of thinking, Carl Jung was a spiritual figure who showed us a way of connecting to the hidden workings of God, humanity, and nature. He is best known as a scientist and researcher in psychology who saw a connection between religious and other myths and the structure of the psyche. I believe Jungian spirituality can be incorporated into any pathway of journeying to God.

My own immersion into a Jungian search for God began in 1975 when I attended an **Ira Progoff** workshop on intensive journal keeping. This three-day workshop was held in Maryland with Ira Progoff as the presenter. Ira Progoff was an American psychotherapist best known for his development of the Intensive Journal Method while at Drew University. His main interest was in depth-psychology and particularly the humanistic adaptation of Jungian ideas to the lives of ordinary people. He founded Dialogue House in New York City to help promote his method. His workshop taught me to use a journal as a foundation for my search to become a balanced, creative expression of who I am.

This journal had several sections each devoted to different aspects of one's life. There were sections for logging night dreams, daytime fantasies, life memories, and in-depth meditations with wisdom figures from one's life. In this journal keeping process, I logged dreams, hopes, aspirations, failures, and fantasies. Through the use of **active imagination,** I **dialoged** with wisdom figures from within my own history.

One such wisdom figure was my maternal grandmother who lived a rural lifestyle in Elton, Louisiana. Elton was a small farming community of about 2000 people. Granny, as a farmer's wife, dedicated her life to love, generosity and simplicity. When I met her, she was a short, quiet, happy, gray-haired woman who often embraced her grandchildren. Her husband had died some years earlier and her only son ran the farm. She could most frequently be found in her kitchen around a sink that had rust water stains draining down the inside of it. Weekly, Mama would take all eight children to visit Granny Lodie. Walking up the sidewalk to the porch of her old two-story farmhouse, running into her arms, I would bury my head in her lap and embrace her with joy. Cookie dough from her apron often greeted my joy with its sweetness. Granny Lodie did not speak much, but in her quiet, loving gestures she served to teach me that there is a feminine way of nourishing life that often goes unseen. Her humble way of encountering others, especially her grandchildren, was always a warm and positive experience. She died when I was twenty-one, after a long battle with cancer.

In my journal, I logged these memories of her kitchen, her apron, and the taste of cookie dough. I meditated often on memories of her embracing me as a toddler. I would imagine and dwell on these memories and let them expand into fantasy of her speaking to me about my hurts in life and how to engage suffering with gentleness and humility. Granny Lodie set the foundation for my later understanding of God as feminine. Her love and wisdom has always been available to me through active imagination and journal keeping,

Intensive journal keeping and reading of Jungian psychology, as it applied to my journey, has been a part of my lifestyle ever since that workshop with Ira Progoff. It opened me to a way of life I call Jungian spirituality. Journaling, active imagination, and dream work have enabled healing of my bi-polar mental illness common to my family heritage.

There were distant relatives who were diagnosed with schizophrenia and manic-depressive illness. I don't recall meeting these relatives, only hearing about them from my father who often told us we had mental illness in our genetic makeup. I even think some of my father's proneness to anger and rage was rooted in an unstable inner identity. But his position of authority as a father and a community leader left him with no one to challenge his rough approach to life. I know from my mother that he often regretted his spontaneous frustrations and rage toward others who disagreed with his beliefs. But he never gained good expression of this negative side in his nature.

A Jungian approach to my life required incorporating seemingly demonic forces from within and without, causing me to experience the Dark side of God. The Dark side of God is that part of God that is unknown or unfathomed by us, like the dark side of the moon. Our imagination can run wild with fear when we speculate on this dark side. It is necessary to embrace the dark and difficult experiences in the soul and daily life in order to be initiated into this spiritual journey. Reading Monika Wikman's book, *Pregnant Darkness*, supported this assumption for me. Using the symbolic meaning and processes of philosophical **alchemy** and individual stories, she showed how it is in the dark and difficult experiences of life that we discover the real gold nuggets we need for living.

The Jungian path of which I speak brings me in contact with the evolving, incarnating dimensions of God and Self as found in my life story. It is a becoming process, an individuating journey, where I discover and fulfill my personal purpose for living, standing out from within the culture of my birth. Individuation is the lifelong process defined by Jung, through which a person uses dream work to understand the Self, and bring their conscious will and daily life expressions into service of that unfolding image. In an individuation process, one is challenged to resolve conflicts arising at life's transitional stages such as adolescents to adulthood, adult middle life and old age. At each transition, one becomes more completely expressive of his or her uniqueness by developing the weaknesses and strengths identified at each stage.

This process requires many facets for its evolving purposes to unfold. I had to develop a lifestyle that noted the importance of dreams, fantasies, memories, and concrete reality. Using the disciplines of dream work with a trained Jungian therapist, active imagination, and growing awareness for what Jung called **synchronicity,** I worked with the **primary material** of my soul.

Synchronicity happens when the unconscious and conscious worlds validate each other with an experience of a mutual expression, sort of like two things happening at once from two different worlds. Synchronicity gives direction and emphasis to the path we choose each day. These moments of two worlds impacting each other are not seen as coincidence. But they are seen as the result of combined waves of energy, from both the conscious and unconscious dimensions, purposely acting on each other. An example would be having a dream one night and then the next day, experiencing it in a concrete event.

Utilizing art, dance, play and other creative ways of handling the basic, difficult and undeveloped traits of my personality (the primary material), I discovered a unique life story, born from a journey with many crossroads and dangerous twists and turns. The difficult and weaker aspects of my personality had to be scrutinized, tolerated and kneaded until they actually showed themselves as strengths and balance for the whole of me. An example of this is how my weakness of depressive tendencies turned out to become avenues for insightful, intuitive reasoning.

Mental illness aggravated but was also healed through my encounter with the disciplines of a Jungian spirituality. In my early adult years, I used Jungian principles but without a therapist or coach. This led to deceptions and assumptions about myself and life that were misguided, such as when I attempted suicide. In a later chapter, I will elaborate on this example of a misunderstanding of a fantasy. These deceptions made my journey especially difficult yet in the end dynamically fruitful with the help of a guide. I know of others who live a Jungian way without encountering mental illness. Though unavoidable for me, mental illness is not a requirement for this way of life. In fact, I think the Jungian way's ultimate purpose is to protect one from the **splits with reality** inherent in the **neuroses** that often plague human existence. It is an approach to life anyone can use but a guide is essential.

I cannot stress enough the importance of a guide for one's journey with this manner of living. Discovering the inner and outer guides for one's life is central to this process, precisely because getting lost on the way is easy and dangerous. Early in the commitment to a Jungian way of seeing, one must seek out a therapist or coach. Finding this coach may be difficult, but it is necessary when using Jungian concepts for healing. As dreams unfold, one also finds inner guides who warn and direct behaviors.

Another concept in depth psychology is that all aspects of the unconscious hold opposing energies, such as light vs. dark, good vs. bad, man vs. woman, child vs. parent, mother vs. father and so on. The interplay of the opposing energies is important in understanding and expressing our most developed self.

For each of us, buried deep within our unconscious is our opposite side, our **shadow** side. Buried here are all the traits and parts of ourselves that over the years we have rejected. Discovering our shadow side and relating to it in order for it to develop and find creative expression is an important challenge in depth psychology. I had to learn that my opinion of myself as a kind and compassionate young woman had to be balanced with the images of the hurtful and mean witch from my shadow side. It was this shadow side that compelled my creative skills in painting and sculpturing to heal the wounds from daily living.

The Self is a central idea and concept of the psyche Jung identified.

If one thinks of God as a multifaceted diamond, the Self would be that particular facet of God that shines from within our own unconscious. It is an expression of our purest and most divine identity that constantly calls out to us from our dreams for authentic lives. I have yet to discover a specific image of the Self in me. Yet the desire for this image energizes me to seek it out with endurance and hope. In someway, this Self in me is a She who is committed to healing Her own wounds and the hurts of others. She seems to be both child and mother.

I have only one tiny view of this lifestyle. My perspective is uniquely mine. The purpose of this book is to express that uniqueness and hopefully show the readers how to engage in this journey in such a way that would develop into a unique perspective for themselves. I encourage you to engage, from your angle, this new way of making one's life authentic, creative, and integrated.

If you find my journey and the topic of depth psychology interesting, I suggest you read and study the works of Carl Jung and his followers. My reference books list may be helpful.

First Phase of my Life: The Innocent Years

Chapter 1: Early Childhood

I cannot speak for long about my childhood. Though it was many years ago, it has always been very close to my consciousness. What I remember may be colored by the journey that followed those innocent, powerless years. But it is my memory, and for that reason, it counts.

I was born the fourth child in a family of eight children to a private-practice physician and his wife, a rural-raised, quiet woman. We lived in Jennings, Louisiana, the governing center for a rural, Southern parish. This two-story older home had three bedrooms, a small kitchen and living room. There was a wonderful swing set in the small backyard where I remember seeing my brothers and sister play with neighborhood children. This home was where I spent my first three years of life. My memories of the earliest years on Shanklin Avenue were of my mother, pregnant, cooking at the stove in a long narrow kitchen. She could sit on a high stool and turn from a pot on the stove where she was stirring food, to the sink on the opposite wall to wash dishes. Seeing her full belly, pregnant for Jake, did not make sense to me, but watching her maneuver this hallway type of space she had for a kitchen captured my fancy. She was always able to stir up a delicious pot of food from any space, for any number of people. She was a great cook.

Connected to this memory of her is the clear memory of me, climbing down a stair from the second floor, with my heart racing as I began this endeavor, all alone. The vital energy of this memory sticks with me today. Every time I begin a new endeavor, my heart races with excitement, hope and expectation as I face a daunting task before me.

I did not always have a diagnosis of bipolar mental illness, but even as a toddler I perceived the world through more than one sense, or from more than one angle. A stairwell, for a toddler in diapers, yet unable to walk alone, is both challenge and invitation. It filled me with foreboding, yet with intuitive expectation. I could see the long narrow stair steps with high handrails. I intuitively felt excited about this as a dangerous but fun place that invited me to the thrill of an accomplishment. At this young age, I had not yet learned to favor either side of this double-edged invitation. I tackled the stair and have no memory of help or falls, only the exhilaration of the moment stays with me. I enjoyed this world on Shanklin Avenue with my sensate perceptions and my intuitive nature. This innocent lack of fear that propelled me down the stair was to vanish from my life and self-concept. Soon fear became the guiding force in my personality and childhood. Intuition became the main way I perceived my world while my sensate perceptions dulled due to the harshness of my developing childhood.

There is one memory in particular from these early years on Shanklin Avenue that was and is a source of great consolation and hope. While playing in the backyard near or under the back porch, I cut my knee on a piece of green glass from a broken 7-up bottle. My mother bandaged my knee and said to me while wiping my tears, "Everything is going to be okay." Her simple gesture and words brought me peace and comfort. Because of the scar from this injury, I have always been able to touch my knee and hear her message of hope and comfort. These early years, with my mother, built in me a solid foundation for a journey that was to become difficult and treacherous.

We moved from this home in town when I was three or four to a setting with ten acres of land on the outskirts of town on Lake Arthur Avenue. The house was white with black shutters and roof. It had a screened-in front porch and a large concrete paved area that surrounded the house on two sides. Oak trees and tall pines in the front and back yard were especially inviting. My first moments in the new home were marked by challenge. As we drove in the long driveway, I leaned onto the front seat, while standing on the back seat. I was so excited about this new home for us and I screamed with joy, right into my father's ear. Daddy sharply yelled and raised his hand to me, forcing me to quiet and sit down. This event left me deeply marked by shame and guilt for feelings of excitement and anticipation. This is my first memory of wounding by my father and it has stayed with me for most of my lifetime.

Fire played a big part in my early years. One of my older brothers, Fred, set fire to the hammock in the backyard that first day at our new home. Fred was a wiry, energetic boy that always pushed the limits in play. It seems he had a strong need to control life and others. He often was forceful in getting his brothers and sisters to do what he wanted. While the parents did their business about the new house, Fred and I investigated the spacious back yard. A swing set was larger than the one on Shanklin Avenue and the hammock with fringe was brand new. Telling me to watch, Fred took out a box of matches and set fire to this fringe. I felt frightened by my father's harshness and my brother's bully behaviors.

When he was three, Fred set a fire under my crib. He often expressed to my parents his desire for the fire trucks he frequently heard pass on busy Shanklin Avenue to come to his home. Choosing to set the fire under my crib must have been his only way of dealing with the powerlessness he felt with a new baby sister in his life. Fortunately enough, Mama smelled smoke and put it out before anything more than a black spot was made on the floor. The burning hammock on Lake Arthur Avenue was the second incident with flames. My brother was fascinated with the power of this element.

When I was six or seven, Fred started burning paper near the gas tank of our family automobile as I watched, unaware of the potential for disaster. The family was working in a garden on the back of the property while Fred and I had wandered off to investigate other things. When my father confronted us, Fred convinced me to take responsibility for this dangerous act.

To teach us the danger of fire and to pressure my brother into confessing his role in the incident, my father placed me in a ring of flames. Terrified, I was motionless before the flames and their heat. The final outcome of this lesson escapes my memory. But fear of destructive burning remains in my consciousness today.

I remember an overbearing father, whose love and attention I desired, but never seemed to be able to secure except in harsh discipline. I developed a fear of anything new or challenging. Shyness took over my adventurous nature. My father's vision of parenthood was mostly to challenge his young offspring. If that meant setting me in a ring of fire to teach me not to play with it, then that was what he did. The circle of flames he set around me was too overwhelming for my childhood innocence to absorb and incorporate in any healthy way.

Fear of my father and sadness are the most remembered feelings I have of my childhood. Somehow my desires to wander in thought and emotion, and my identification with the underdog in all stories of life were disgusting to him. He tried his hardest to correct these natural impulses in me. Frequently I would bring sick or stray animals home to be nursed back to health. Daddy would tell me there was no hope for the creature and send it away from my mothering nature. There is an understanding in my family that World War II, in which my father served, changed his personality and forced him into this harsh mode of fathering. I know his family heritage was marked by this concept of a bullish attitude toward the challenges of life and the responsibilities of authority positions. His mother and sister both had demanding personalities.

There was a passionately alive side to my father's nature. The expression in him of the Bull archetype, with its powerful god-like stature was attractive and magnetic, but it was only a tiny view of the great unconscious power my family inherited in its connection to the mythological figure of the Minotaur. This figure with his half-man, half-bull body was the god that youths were sacrificed to, by condemning them to the bull's labyrinth and the death that was its outcome. These young people were lost in this maze and eventually eaten by the bull.

My father and the atmosphere of my childhood home did not honor the feminine that nurtures imagination and emotion. He chose to restrict, trap or destroy expression of the feminine. Daddy had a tremendous desire to honor and cherish my mother, but he did not trust her intuitive, feeling skills and she eventually chose not to trust these in herself. Though Mama felt a need to hold and rock her children from their infancy, Daddy was convinced this gesture would spoil a child's growth. He often instructed my mother on how to be a mother, but I never heard him ask her how she would like to mother.

Daily, Daddy would hug, kiss, or caress Mama and could not pass her by without at least touching her in a tender way. But when he harshly disciplined his children, she was not allowed to follow her instinct to comfort and protect them. When Father would spank us, I would look to my mother for compassion and see pain in her eyes, as she would turn from my gaze. Thus I grew up feeling abandoned by my mother's protective nurturing. I eventually grew up unskilled at protecting myself.

An example of my lack of self protection can be seen in a first grade memory of a boy who pressured me to kiss him. When he finally caught me, the principal of this four-room, rural school witnessed the kiss. Appalled, she immediately made us embarrass ourselves by insisting we kiss in front of every classroom. Rather than object, cry, or refuse to participate in this punishment, I submitted and never told my parents of the incident. I felt confused and ashamed, and feared their judgment of me.

Though I worshipped and adored my parents as a child, I grew up convinced that I was not good enough to merit their love and attention. As children all our needs for clothing, sleep, food, school, and church were met. Yet, there was an emotional abandonment by my parents, which led me to believe I was not a worthy person. My emotional needs became trapped in a vessel of introversion and withdrawal. I learned the daily functions of living and getting along with others, but feared and withdrew from all intimacy.

To this day, I do not understand my father's contempt for my compassionate, contemplative nature, because these were values that marked his inner life many times. Daily, he would rise early to prayerfully dedicate himself to the service of God as a physician, husband and father. He began every meal with prayer and often blessed his children as they grew in stature and behavior by praying openly in thanksgiving for them. He took a three-day weekend off every year to isolate in prayer at a Christian retreat. On three different occasions, he shared our home, for months at a time, with homeless teenagers. But when I took up concerns for weak animals and people, he either failed to notice or simply belittled my efforts.

My father showed disrespect for my sensitive nature by always demanding that I control my emotions. When I cried over disappointing events, he would say to me, "Stop that crying." He desperately needed me to "grow up" and mature. I sometimes wonder now that perhaps he sensed in me the fragile nature I carried. I think he feared the fate of this natural aspect of my personality, perhaps seeing a future doomed to harm and failure. He even said to me on one occasion that he saw my future as a "bag lady" or misfit, living on the margins of society. Unfortunately, he could not see the courage, perseverance, determination, and belief I had within me that would ultimately lead to wholeness and integrity and a solid place in society.

I did not develop a strong emotional connection to my mother. She was consumed with the demands of home life for a family of ten. This lack of connection to her left me abandoned to my intuitive imagination. This inner trait served me well, securing hope for life, in the midst of a reality I found either too brutal from my father or too bland and boring due to the busyness of my mother. Though we have pictures of her reading to my oldest brother, I have no memory of my mother's nurturing nature towards me. Mother's significant role of cleaning, clothing, and feeding these eight children left little room for her to mirror our unique worthiness and calls in life. A parent can mirror a child's worthiness by frequent eye-to-eye contact and verbal affirmation of the child's behaviors and temperament. I have no memory of this from Mama or Daddy. The wound in my soul made by this feeling-absence of my mother was probably more tragic than the harsh discipline of my father. Perhaps if I had had a close example of how to deal with emotions and nurturing, I could have dealt with my father's demanding temperament. My Granny Lodie was the closest example of emotional nurturing, but she was often disregarded as too simple and unimportant. We were not encouraged to be like Granny Lodie since she never achieved any greatness as a professional person. My mother did not value Granny Lodie's life as a farmer's wife since it was this lifestyle Mama wanted to escape. I did not learn at an early age how to be feminine, or to trust and be proud of this identity. It would take years of struggle with this abandonment before I could value emotions and relationships as primary and central to my self-expression.

My intuitive nature developed a strong connection to the spiritual possibilities in every moment. I wandered in my imagination with God I found in nature, sunsets, the Milky Way and the wind in the trees. I remember running to get under the rays of light streaming from the sun through the clouds in our back field, hoping to get a blessing from God I believed was there. I would dance with the wind as it blew my dress along with the limbs on the great Loblolly pines in our back yard. Playing in the clover grass under the swing set fascinated me as I made jewelry for my wrists and neck from the flowers that bloomed there in the spring and summer. A contemplative, compassionate intuition grew strong all through my childhood, disconnecting me from the brutal, logical and practical energies of my parents that aimed to contain and guide the eight wild natures within my family of brothers and sisters.

Shyness took over my exploring nature, and introversion tried to shape me into an ideal pleasing child that never wandered far and always obeyed the rules. I had a knack for making people laugh but often it was by using myself as the butt of a joke. With visitors to our home whether children or adults, I chose not to interact in any significant way. Though I played games with brothers and sisters and neighborhood children, I got close to no one. I did have a desire for closeness. I remember lying to a friend in the third grade that I had a Girl Scout troop that met in my home. I wanted to convince this friend to come to play with me. When she showed up for the meeting I was speechless. She never came to play with me again and I did not invite her anymore.

Introversion and shyness had a positive side. There was a game I played as a child when sent to bed. I played this game to help me cope with frequent tears and fears of the dark that I experienced every night. When afraid or crying myself to sleep, a little Tinkerbell type fairy would come to me in my imagination and catch my tears in a flask. Then she would have me drink the tears to gain strength. She was a consoling figure from my **subconscious** that enabled me to get through many disappointments as a child and somehow preserved the core of my true identity as a sensitive, feeling, feminine presence in the world, as I am today.

Years into adulthood, reflecting on my childhood and the myth of the Minotaur, I was able to associate the bullish temperament of my father with this myth. I learned of the story of the Minotaur from a psychology teacher when I was in graduate school. This study revealed certain concepts that explain some beliefs about my life. It is as though the myth of the Minotaur was the controlling archetype in my childhood home. I associate the labyrinth and the bull in this myth with the circuitous path of pure logic when it functions without the grounding guidance of relatedness and emotions. By pure logic, I refer to the thinking or analytical skills we all have. This logic can be in direct opposition to the feeling functions we also posses. Bullish thinking, without an emotional connection to its subject, can create a maze causing one to wander in critique or analysis, never achieving an adequate resolution for the situation.

For example, in gardening, one can love the earth and its products without knowledge of the science that explains how sun and water, earth and seed combine to produce flowers. A loving gardener watches and learns how to ensure that plants grow. A scientist, without this love, can explain well how these forces work and function, but without relating to them on an emotional level, will stay in his or her ivory tower of thought and critique, never becoming a successful gardener.

When logic is primary and functions without regard for feelings and emotional relatedness, it is concerned with theory rather than down to earth reality, thus belittling real people and situations. Science without heart can be very destructive. This was the approach to life my father chose for himself and his family. And like the story of the Minotaur, the children were regularly sacrificed to this concept.

It is interesting to note that in the myth of the Minotaur, it was a woman's ball of yarn that enabled the hero to find his way into the labyrinth, kill the Minotaur and find his way out again. It took the feminine connected to the masculine for the myth to complete itself and for the hero to be successful.

Though my parents were a loving and dedicated couple, there was a split between the masculine and feminine energies. Daddy's authoritative rule with Mama's subservient position created an imbalance to which my nature was sensitive. It was this split that contributed to my adult complications in integrating these two opposites in my life and personality.

Chapter II: School and College Years:

As I grew into grade school and college years I did well, but school meant little to me. I went off to college hoping to become a veterinarian, and to find a husband, married life and many children. A part of me identified with the loving intimacy between my parents and the chaos of eight little ones running around. I always nurtured these dreams of husband and many children in childhood play.

I soon gave up the desire to become a veterinarian because I mistakenly thought it was not a very Christian vocation. It seemed I should give my life for people instead of animals. As a child, I was always taught by my parents to cherish a Christian call to sacrifice self for others. I loved and felt dedicated to the well being of animals, but we were taught that they did not have a soul and were not worthy of an emotional commitment. I always did, and still do, have a special place in my heart for animals. As a child, I even tried to create a mud home for frogs one summer. I struggled at this creative endeavor, but all the frogs hopped away, leaving me with a sense of failure. My inner world never invited others into its efforts or decision-making.

As a freshman in college at the University of Southwestern Louisiana in Lafayette, I chose to change my major from a pre-vet curriculum to nursing. This school was about an hour drive from our home and had about 10,000 students. I felt lost in this setting but enjoyed the adventure of being away from home. Nursing school was not hard for me academically. I studied every day and made good grades, but learned little about the art of healing. I was afraid of the clinical aspect of nursing school. It seemed it focused on the cold concept of precision and perfection that left little room for the development of a compassionate role as a healing instrument.

In my rotations through the nursing lab and hospital setting, I learned techniques and procedures that were aimed at curing illness. I was not taught how to encounter the suffering patient on a personal level or how to deal with all the emotions I saw in the eyes of my patients each day. My own needs had to be buried and denied as I learned to identify and control the physical needs of sick people. Techniques and procedures were the logical tools I had to master in the healing of a person's illness.

Frequently, after a day's rotation in the hospital, I would walk home crying. I was overwhelmed by the fear and sadness I saw in patients, while I dealt with my own inadequacies in handling tubes, needles, and machines needed in their care. My instructors were more concerned with how I calculated the drip-rate on an intravenous infusion than how well I identified and responded to a patient's fears of dying. I never really became comfortable with this concept of nursing education. I longed to be a healing instrument but did not identify with the tools taught in traditional clinical nursing.

In college, I lived off-campus with my brothers and sisters and was isolated from campus life. Daddy had four children in undergraduate school at the University of Southwestern Louisiana in Lafayette, and two in medical school in New Orleans at the same time. It was financially better for him to purchase a house near the campus in Lafayette than pay for dormitory living. I lived the four years at USL with two older and two younger siblings.

As brothers and sisters, we helped each other deal with the freedom away from parents, a new and strange environment, and the peer pressures associated with this world. We shared meals and provided for each other a quiet place for study. We laughed together at our sometimes-foolish choices for weekend fun such as drinking too much at the nearby pub.

There was a hardship living with family. I was never exposed to the socialization process with college peers in dorms or sororities. I made few friends and dated infrequently.

One man I dated, Richard, asked me to marry him, and I was in love with him, but my father did not approve of our relationship. I had met Richard in my senior year in high school at a classmate's home. He was twenty-one and I was seventeen. We could not date when I was in high school, as Daddy did not allow me to date yet. But we did meet secretly at the local ice cream shop on the weekends and became close. In college I had more freedom and did begin to date him regularly. His maturity and older nature attracted me and his ability to make me laugh was fun. He worked as a bookkeeper for a local business. His family background was poor financially and mostly unknown to me.

Daddy did not trust him. My father's role as a physician made him aware of something scandalous about Richard or his family. Daddy wanted to protect me. Because he was bound by professional confidentiality, he never shared this scandal with me, but it was always forefront in his mind whenever we spoke of Richard. Daddy often would say to me, "I know about this man, and he is not good for you." I can't imagine how a father copes with such an experience. Daddy was torn by professional demands and yet his desire to protect me forced him to breach these demands at least in part. At one point when I was a junior in college, I was told I could not date Richard anymore. I chose to secretly see him one more time.

One weekend, all my brothers and sisters went back to our home in Jennings to be with the rest of the family, while I stayed in Lafayette to study. I made plans to meet Richard for a date on that Saturday, against my father's wishes. My older brother heard of my scheduled date. Feeling responsible for my obedience to the rules of my father, he told Daddy of my plans.

As I waited for Richard to pick me up, I was confronted by my brothers who came in, packed up my belongings, forced me into the family car and transported me back to our family home in Jennings. I had to face my father's punishment for disobeying him. Enduring my father's accusations that I was a "slut" was not as difficult as the separation from Richard. Saddened by the loss of this encounter with Richard, I worried about what he thought of the empty house when he came to pick me up. I was not allowed to return to school until the next semester. I took incompletes in my summer classes.

I returned to college after that summer. A few months later, Richard had a meeting with my father, after which we were allowed to date openly. I was not permitted to attend this meeting and never did learn of its contents or how the issue of our dating was resolved. But the relationship did not last long after the freedom to date was given. Eventually, Richard chose to marry another, probably because of the challenges my father placed on the relationship.

My father's protective guarding of my social life left me with a lack of a developed instinctive and sensual connection to life. Because shyness was my way of interacting with the world, I failed to respond to any of Richard's advances. He was a fun-loving person and often tried to engage me with conversation, playfulness, and romance. I felt awkward with these interactions, and I suppose, to him I was cold and unresponsive. My introversion and my father's pressure on the relationship led to its end.

In my heart, I loved Richard's playfulness and romantic gestures. When we danced, I felt rocked and loved, touched by tenderness. But I could not bring myself to share these feelings. Richard grew tired of my emotional introversion yet frequent talk about religion and the social justice issues of the sixties. On one occasion he even suggested I become a nun. He opted for an earthy, sensuous woman, who was sexy and responsive. It was a very painful loss for me.

Richard had the component of playfulness and humor that I needed from the masculine to open me to life. In the twenty years that followed his rejection, I learned he lacked the insight into my shy nature that was crucial for a successful connection between us. Though I grieved the loss of him in my later life, it was more the loss of the role of wife and mother that saddened my future. Richard held out to me the possibility of my childhood dream of being a mama with lots of children. When I was three, my parents asked me what I would like to be when I grew up. I replied, "I want to be a mama with big ninnies and lots of children." This dream was never to become true.

Another event in my college years took decades to integrate into my personality. I was raped while on a blind date. A fellow nursing student invited me to meet her brother. She said he wanted to get to know me. She set the date up for one Saturday afternoon during my senior year.

What I remember of this event is vague and dream-like due to drugs he gave me. The young man picked me up around three p.m. to go to a barbeque with his friends in the countryside. On the way there, he was smoking a pipe and offered it to me. He told me it had marijuana in it. Thinking this was like a glass of wine or a beer, I said yes, not knowing he had laced it with something stronger. Almost immediately, I was in an imaginary world and unconscious until the next morning. The images from this dream-state involved lights following me, airplanes overhead, and a forest in the distance. These few images are the only memories I have of the fourteen hours this drug was in control of my life. What I do remember is marked by fear and confusion.

At five a.m., I woke to awareness with him on top of me, inside me, and felt myself to be nude. In horror, I shoved him off of me and went to the bathroom. There, in total fear, shock and shame, I wondered where I was and how I could get home. Part of me thought I had brought all of this on myself. In a mental fog, I searched for my clothes and asked to be taken home. Once there, I went to bed and into a deep sleep.

When I woke at eleven-thirty a.m., I found the bruises on my thighs and was consciously aware of the violence that had been done to me. Though I was still in shock, I went to the phone, called this man, and in trembling fear, told him I wanted nothing to do with him or his lifestyle. Immediately I decided no one must find out what I had done in accepting the pipe, or of the incident that followed. In guilt, I buried the whole encounter.

At a time in my life when I should have been on fire with anger and defense of my innocence, I shamefully hid from this experience. At the time of the rape I was so ashamed of this event that I hid from it. But later in life I made the connection of it to my life story. This rape was part of the routine I had come to know between the masculine and feminine. My childhood taught me that feminine feelings and innocence were not important, and that harsh masculine logic was the appropriate response to every situation. I thought, in dealing with this rape, masculine logic should dominate feminine feelings. My logic said I chose to smoke the marijuana. Therefore I was guilty and deserved the consequences, even though the child in me felt violated. I told no one of my experience and shoved it out of my consciousness. In my shock, fear and mostly shame, I tried to deny it ever happened.

Over the years, I came to realize I had used this same logic to shove out of my consciousness the violation of my vulnerable feminine nature by my father's aggressive disciplines. Prior to this realization, I lived many years as a young adult thinking I had a normal, healthy childhood home.

This rape, though it was a real event, has come to stand as a symbol of something that went on in my mind for years before this actual rape occurred. This image of rape seems to describe three events in my life: my father's aggressive discipline, my actual rape in college and later the overwhelming of my consciousness by a psychosis. There was a compulsive game I would play as a child and even as an older adult. In my imagination, every time I passed an open driveway, I would visualize a long stick thrusting into the empty driveway. This fantasy was much like the common compulsion to not step on a crack in the pavement as one walked. The image of the driveway and the stick could be linked to a rape experience of the hostile masculine as it overtakes the open feminine. My father's severe disciplines, particularly when he harshly punished me as we drove the long driveway into our new home on Lake Arthur Avenue, taught me that critical logic was more important than vulnerable feelings. Daddy's aggressive temperament coupled with this college rape event and my psychotic event later in life, all seem to be related experiences. In all three experiences, I was forced to deal with powers greater than myself that forced me to be a victim.

Today, in my own psyche, I associate my logic-oriented thinking skills with my masculine energy. I connect my feeling, value-oriented nature with the feminine. My harsh, objective, logic-oriented thinking had little respect for my open, embracing feminine emotions. As a young adult, I believed I had no rights or value as a person and seldom acted on my feelings. The disrespect for my spiritual and emotional side that marked my world was in direct opposition to my child-like nature of devotion to the vulnerable and infinite.

This tension between masculine and feminine energies created great conflict within me, contributing to my introversion. Later in my life as an adult, I would be forced to deal with these opposing energies of the masculine and feminine.

The psychological rape of my childhood, the physical rape from my college years, and the later mental rape in my adult years by my unconscious energies in psychosis, all forcefully demanded I be a victim in this world of reality. In time, I chose to be a celebrant of the mysteries between the thinking-masculine and feeling-feminine opposites in life.

Second Phase of my Life:
Experimenting with Identity

Chapter III: Navy Nurse

In my memory, I am sitting on an airplane leaving New Orleans airport, bound for Providence, RI and officer's training school in the Navy. It is a typical, hot and humid summer day in 1971. I have graduated with a Bachelor of Science in Nursing and I am twenty-one years old. Wearing a dark blue dress with white polka dots, I feel stunning. This flight is marked by an eagerness for a new life filled with hope. I am so excited about being freed of my father's hold over my life.

The decision to join the Navy was made with the expectation of escaping my painful youth. I wanted desperately to leave Louisiana and the tight reins of my family's influence, but I knew as a young woman, I could not move far away alone. That morning of my first airplane ride marked the beginning of a whole new chapter of my life as I expected to find a new family and sense of belonging in the Navy. I first saw the poster advertising the Navy on the school campus in my junior year. My wish to join was denied by my father as he felt only disturbed women such as "lesbians" joined the armed forces. But I persisted in my interest and finally in my senior year, he consented to allow me this adventure.

Little did I understand, at this point in my life, that the Bull and its threatening, trampling, overrunning approach would remain deep within my personality make-up.

The professional world of nursing and my father seemed captivated by the crystal clear logic of scientific reasoning with little appreciation of intuition and feelings, seemingly all head and no heart. I did not understand, as I transitioned to independence, that I would have to one day stand and face this one-sided bullish logic and transform its brute energy into creative strength.

Officer's Training School in Providence, Rhode Island did not make a big impression on me except for the excitement of being in a new territory and climate. I had to wear a sweater sometimes in the middle of July, unheard of in my Louisiana days. What I remember mostly was the inspections of our rooms to be sure nothing was out of order, including a misplaced hair on the bathroom floor. My roommate was so upset by this hair when the inspectors found it that she almost cried. I said to her, "It's just a hair!" We began to laugh at some of the ways the military had of creating an obedient, cohesive, responsible organization of women officers. We learned of the importance of saluting the correct people and not to fraternize with corpsman. But nothing in this twelve-week course seemed to grab me emotionally. I did choose three possible duty stations, including Portsmouth, Virginia, the Great Lakes area in Illinois, or San Diego. I anxiously awaited my orders and was pleasantly surprised when I got my first choice. The only thing I knew about the Virginia Naval Base was that the hospital had a great neuro-surgical ward and I had excelled in school in this area of study. The study of neurology and surgical interventions was complicated material and I found it fascinating. I grasped it fairly easily.

My initial years as an officer and a nurse, away from the overpowering masculine influence of my father, was a time for me to develop a sense of ownership for life and its responsibilities.

Once settled at my first duty station at the Portsmouth Naval Base, I chose to establish a home off base with another Navy nurse. Making our apartment into a home was easy and fun, but my shyness and isolation continued. Frequently, my roommate and other nurses from her ward at the hospital would get together off base for a party. Corpsman from the hospital were always invited. The nurses and corpsmen were all paired off and I felt like a fifth wheel, usually making an excuse for not attending. I would venture off by myself to explore the nearby rural areas or the fields of trees near our apartment complex. I wrote a lot about my daily life and wondered in my imagination about my future. I confided my deepest self to no one, because I was somehow unaware of it. My shy, cautious nature kept me from connecting to my real self or that of others. Only my childhood dream of being a wife and mother stayed with me consciously.

For the most part, my years of active duty were marked by a feeling of not fitting in: loneliness and yearning for a beginning to my lifelong-dream of being a homemaker, longing for someone to see this identity within me and call it forth, looking for an adequate masculine response to my presence. I dated but never connected emotionally to anyone who wanted me. The men I did connect with were either not available because of lack of interest in me, or only wanted a sexual partner without commitment.

My time on active duty never involved me passionately. As I neared the end of my Navy commitment, the commanding officer of my duty station invited me to handle a special project. I assumed her motive was to entice me to extend my time with the Navy. She saw in me potential for leadership with compassion and wanted to capitalize on this energy. This officer asked me to survey the needs of dying patients and the hospital team's ability to respond.

Visiting the dying overwhelmed me with emotion and I felt intimidated by my poorly developed organizational and relationship skills. Each day I would visit terminally ill patients and interview them to assess their emotional and physical needs.

One morning at four a.m. lab-draw time, I was visiting a dying woman whose abdomen was filled with cancer. She had exhausted all treatment, yet the doctor wanted a blood sample for further testing. I cannot forget her tears as she suffered silently, enduring the needles digging for a vein in her shriveled arm. She seemed to beg, "Why is this necessary? What good will it do?" I felt helpless and inadequate before her, as I had no answer. I felt deeply the injustice of dying in a hospital setting.

My inability to relate well to suffering patients and my lack of defense for their emotional needs made me tremble in the face of their struggles. I abandoned the assigned project before its completion.

During these years with the Navy, I sought out volunteer work with the Catholic Church serving the needs of the poor in Portsmouth, Virginia. Here I found the values of compassion, commitment, and contemplation. With nuns and lay volunteers, I worked in the homes of poor elderly couples, and with families that lived in poor neighborhoods and housing projects. Alongside the poor, I assisted them in the daily struggles of their lives. We had a special program called Operation Santa Claus. In this effort, we collected toys from neighboring churches and distributed them on Christmas Eve to the homes of families we knew were not going to have a Christmas due to financial hardships. The joy and smiles on the faces of the parents and children as they met Santa Claus in their homes and opened their gifts was priceless and memorable for me.

Because prayer was a daily routine of my Christian life as a child, it planted within me the desire to dedicate myself to God and helping others. My parents had a strong active faith, having converted to the Catholic religion as young adults when they married. They took this conversion seriously and sought to live out the teachings of the Church. But more than that, they talked about this faith easily. Though my father taught me to question the teachings and rules of the Pope, he also taught me of the holiness and wholeness one can attain through the sacraments over a lifetime. They chose weekly confession, daily mass, and the rosary as a family as their rituals for getting emotionally close to God. They tried to teach us of the importance of this caring and emotional commitment to God that would change us as we grew into better people. I learned to enjoy religious practices but more importantly I learned to love God and seek His presence in my daily activities through reflection and acts of kindness. With this passion for a God-centered life, I came to encounter the rituals of faith with meaning. Without this focus, religious practices would be empty, meaningless behaviors.

I carried this passion for a fruitful spiritual life all through my Navy career, but felt inadequate as a nurse. The doctors on the ward praised my knowledge and skills as a neuro-nurse but I always felt inadequate in managing the mixture of nursing duties involved in direct patient care. I had poor organizational skills and was still frightened of technical equipment.

There were two men, Charles and William, who almost kept me from saying yes to a desire I felt to become a nun. Charles was a corpsman who was stationed at Portsmouth Naval Hospital where I worked. He was handsome to me with red hair and mustache even though he was not tall like I preferred in most men. He was about 5' 8". We socialized extensively outside of work, and I secretly had hopes that he would one day make a romantic gesture towards me that would develop into married life. But this never happened.

Remembering Charles is easy. He taught me to make angels in the first snow I ever experienced. I could talk with him about my playful wanderings in forests and talking to trees in the field near my apartment. We would sit on the harbor wall of Portsmouth Shipyard; hang our feet over the edge at night when all was dark and quiet. We were intimately alone. We watched the cargo ships slip into the harbor, passing silently in the dark, ghost-like. In our imagination, they carried a crew of dead men with many treasures from their worldly journeys.

We would talk about the youthful feeling of being unfinished, unexpressed and having an immense sense of a vacancy or void within us. This pregnant void was like a profound longing filled with potential and hope, but somehow vague and empty. He would write poems that put me on a pedestal or spoke of me as a heroine. I tended to ignore or turn from these images, somehow feeling so unworthy and ashamed of that identity.

I secretly longed for a reciprocal, romantic connection with Charles, and even though we slept together, we were more like children and siblings rather than lovers. We lived intuitively with the sense that a sexual connection was taboo. I found out many years later that Charles was possibly gay or perhaps bi-sexual as I frequently saw him date women. But I learned in the 1990's that he was dying of AIDS. I took his choice of sexual orientation as a rejection and felt sad when I heard this news. I can only imagine the personal struggle he must have gone through in the Navy trying to discover and live out his understanding of sexuality. It became obvious to me that he did not see me as a sexual partner, perhaps more just a dear friend for the while it lasted.

In looking back, over the years, I lost touch with Charles, but never stopped longing for him. He represented a betwixt-between period in my life that was full of imaginative death, birth, searching, longing and letting go: a period of time that he did not want to pin down with a commitment, at least not with me. With Charles, the playful, imaginative part of me, which wandered in nature with muses from within, was allowed expression. It seems he represents an inner image in me that prefers the imaginative and its freedom over the demands of a concrete reality.

Remembering Charles is like an illusion or fantasy that cannot be understood but only experienced as a real memory of once-dreamt ideals. This relationship served the purpose of connecting me to the archetype of **Hermes** and his great leadership skills in the **night-sea journey**. In Murray Stein's book, *In Mid-Life, A Jungian Perspective*, Hermes is presented as the archetype that is a companion whenever a person is at a crossroads or in a transitional period. Hermes helps us cross the threshold between the conscious and subconscious worlds and leads us with his mysterious presence. Memories of Charles connect me to this impish, trickster, playful archetype. Charles was playful and impish at times. Charles often played tricks on me in a joking manner. Hermes was to surface later in my life and plays an important role in my healing. I think I had projected the energy of this archetype of Hermes onto Charles and wanted intensely for it to be real. I needed in my life the companionship and leadership that the

49

archetype Hermes offers.

My time with Charles seemed trapped in the world of play and imagination without the grounding of a concrete, structured relationship, such as found in a commitment to each other. Yet, we remained friends even years after I left the Navy.

Charles went on years after our time together to become a doctor of psychiatric nursing while my future held mental illness. Somehow these eventual identities were expressed in our connection as friends in the early 1970's. Quoting Pierre Teilhard de Chardin, "…the future enters into us in order to transform itself in us, long before it happens."

In the spring of 1972, after Charles, there was William. He worked in the Portsmouth City Manager's office. He was the only non-Navy man I dated while in the Navy. He was about ten years my senior. William was tall, with soft rounded features that made him gently handsome. He was direct in his assessments of situations and his views on life but never forceful in trying to get others to see his way. We met through the volunteer work program I did for the Catholic Church. William, representing the City Manager's office, had guiding input for our community projects.

From the moment we first met, there was a strong attraction between us. We dated soon after meeting and engaged in a sexual relationship almost immediately. Though we had this attraction, I feared him because he was not my peer; I felt powerless and vulnerable with him. In fact, I even feared pregnancy and married life with him, all the while desiring him.

While I dated William and was still in the Navy, I did extensive volunteer work for the Catholic Church. Dating William, with the sexual arousal we shared, was a direct challenge to my religious upbringing. Sex before marriage, especially resulting in pregnancy, was a scandal for a Catholic woman in strong standing with the Church. I was ashamed to pursue birth control, yet I feared intensely that my sexual relationship with William would lead to pregnancy. My attraction to him left me confronted by these difficult feelings. I was too shy to discuss this with William or anyone. As a follower of nuns and a Christian way of life with the Catholic Church, I felt it was impossible for me to discuss this conflict with my elders or the local priests. I felt sure they would only view me as a harlot or slut as my father had accused me of being. One day I walked for an hour outside of a family planning clinic, contemplating going in, but I just could not bring myself to do it. Birth Control was against my religion and possibly a sin. I was terribly conflicted in my faith and sexuality. My powerless, impressionable feminine and child-like nature could not deal adequately or logically with this inner conflict.

One early morning, after spending the day and night with William in an intimate connection, I asked him to drive me to Hosanna House, a community of Catholic Nuns. William seemed to be in shock, as he had no verbal response to my request. He drove me in the dark early morning hours to this old two-story, eight-bedroom house in a cul-de-sac of a quiet city neighborhood. We did not speak on the trip.

That morning I was torn with emotions of wanting William, yet fearing him. I had two weeks earlier gotten my early-out discharge orders but told no one of my plans to leave the Navy. Confused with emotions, I felt I had to leave William behind along with my duty station I left the Navy after fourteen months on active duty, but remained in the Reserves for three more years.

This abrupt decision-making, and 180-degree turn, was typical of my life in these early adult years. The Bull in me demanded immediate solutions to complex problems, especially when they involved connection and conflict between masculine and feminine energies.

A short time after entering religious life, I gave a speech before the Portsmouth city council hoping to secure grant money for a project in a poor neighborhood. My speech was passionately and exquisitely given. I spoke of the rights of the poor for proper health care and the responsibility of the City to support efforts to bring this health care to their neighborhoods. You could have heard a pin drop in the room while I spoke and applause sounded at the end. William was there. He tried to reach me through the crowd, calling my name, but I purposely evaded him, fearing the dynamism between us. We never discussed the separation between us. Though I saw him once more several months later after I had become a nun, we did not even greet each other with "hello" from the short distance between us on the city street.

My relationship with William was brief but intense. He brought out my inadequacy around men and my fears of sexual energy. I did not realize that in becoming a nun, I was trying to find a space in life to heal from the contempt of my father for all that was fragile in me, the broken engagement, and the rape during my college years. These three encounters from the first phase of my life were unhealed, hurtful wounds that were gaping open deep within my subconscious where I had buried them in order to live and go on in daily life with smiles and hope. This open grave haunted me without my conscious realization of it.

William and the tremendous sexual energy he brought out in me served to confront me face to face with my wounded nature. Relating to him with my whole being was impossible for me. I seemed to separate my body, mind and emotions and was not able to connect all three within myself. I was attracted to him physically, feared him emotionally, but logically and intuitively recognized his temperament as good potential for a husband. But I just could not put all these facets of knowing him together into a direct response from me.

Being with him caused me to tremble as I faced the depth of these wounds, not only in my own history but also in society as I saw it. Around me were over-confident men and struggling women in the separations of classes and cultures that I worked with as a volunteer. Poverty and wealth, success and failure in society spoke to me of the deep wound in the world and in myself. I felt called to heal this wound, which was like a deep crater that divided whom and what I did not know. I was familiar with the thinking of the theologian, de Chardin and his statement about the mystery of society, life and suffering expressed in the words "…to build a mountain, one has to dig a hole." It was as though to me the advances in society were on the backs of the poor. I felt emotionally drawn to the "hole" rather than the "mountain." Somehow I felt that religious life would give me the space needed for facing this wound, this hole. As a nun, I would be directly involved with the journey of the poor and downtrodden to wholeness and integrity, to a better life they sought and struggled to attain. Without realizing it, I too was on a journey from being a downtrodden victim to becoming a whole and integrated human being.

Chapter IV: Catholic Nun

I joined the Sisters for Christian Community immediately after leaving the Navy. The Sisters For Christian Community did not have any traditional training program for someone who wanted to join their order. Most women coming to the order were older and were leaving traditional convents and orders of nuns at a mid-life transition. These women had already had basic training and personality development in whatever religious lifestyles they came from. The significant thing they all had in common was that they were at a crossroads in their lives. They may have been dissatisfied with the traditional lifestyle of a nun or had experienced the death of their husband or perhaps even divorce. These events prompted them to seek a new lifestyle that embodied their spiritual search for a new life. The SFCC order was attractive to women at crossroads. When I joined them in 1972 they already had over 700 women spread out over all continents. The SFCC order had begun in 1970. They were small groups of women who banded together globally through commitments to vows of obedience to the Holy Spirit as It lead them, vows of poverty lived through simplicity rather than a forced lack of ownership of property, and vows of celibacy. Each nun had to decide for herself how she would live out these three vows. The sisters I encountered in Portsmouth did not wear habits and had their own bank accounts. They each worked in an area of life that they were trained in and enjoyed. They each embraced their unique understanding of the Holy Spirit and followed their vision each day, as they felt called to do so. One was a choir director, another an accountant, and another a church parish administrator. Another one worked in a local thrift store.

As a young woman with a BS degree in Nursing but no formal training in the lifestyle of a nun, I was a challenge to how the order would embrace young inexperienced and psychologically undeveloped aspirants to their community. They had no identified training program. In traditional orders there would have been a structured development program for a new member. The sisters in the Portsmouth area felt I only needed to live with them and discover the how and what of convent life through daily living. I chose to live with the sisters at Hosanna House. Their passion for a simple life that was centered on prayer and service attracted me.

Hosanna House was an old two story home located in Portsmouth, Virginia where I had been stationed. Previously it had been a family home with eight bedrooms and two large family rooms. It was nestled in a wooded property on an acre of land in a cul-de-sac of a middle class neighborhood. This home was older than the other homes in the neighborhood and obviously had once been the only home on land that was divided and sold to individuals for a neighborhood development. Hosanna House was secluded yet in a closely nit neighborhood.

My first year at Hosanna House was living with two other nuns, and for a short time, with young runaway girls placed with us from the court system. We provided a home and model for these girls, a feminine way of encountering life's problems. With a shared life marked with structure, play, acceptance and love, we aspired to imprint on these girls a hope-filled way of dealing with the challenges of growing up in a world that did not meet their needs and had imprisoned them. I, too, for the first time in my adult life, was finding a home, a sense of belonging and a new vision for myself.

Katie, one of the thirteen-year-old girls with us, was particularly needy and responded well to the loving, yet disciplined environment we provided. She was a pudgy, shorthaired blond, who ran away from her dysfunctional home where her father beat both her and her mother. Living on the streets, she had been further abused. She had never known nuns before and found our lifestyle interesting. She would sit in on our morning and evening prayers.

Our prayer time was a dedicated hour every morning and evening, centered on worship with songs of praise for God the Father, Jesus the Christ Savior and Servant, and Mary, a creative expression of the feminine side of God and Church. We sang songs and shared prayer. Shared prayer was a simple way of verbalizing out loud and spontaneously, a few words to God as the individual felt called to express at the moment. It was very revealing of one's internal thoughts and feelings regarding the present day experiences. Often these words were expressions of struggles with faith, or praise and petition for one's hopes and desires for the beginning of the day, or gratitude at the end of the day. Morning prayer was called lauds, and evening prayer was vespers. Blessings on the sacredness of the day and the night were a constant theme.

Katie sat in on our prayer sessions with silent respect and seldom shared prayer. When she did speak a prayer, it was simple and revealing of her desire for unity with her family.

One day while we shared cooking responsibilities in the kitchen, she asked a straightforward question. "What makes you not have a man in your life?" When I told her it was our choice, she seemed amazed that women could live without a man. And she seemed pleased to know that this was a possibility.

Katie's inquisitive nature forced me to answer questions I had to face. I felt the loss of my long-hoped-for dreams of marriage and my own children. I longed for both Charles and William to come and save me from my tortured self. Depression over these things drove me for about six months to live alone as an aspirant of the Sisters for Christian Community. As an aspirant, I rented an apartment, worked as a nurse, and began and ended my day with prayer and journal keeping. I was trying to decide on my own if I really wanted to try to become a nun. I had no one to guide me in this search as an aspirant in a traditional order would have had. My journal keeping was my way of tracking my thoughts and feelings about making this decision. I would journal my thoughts and feelings about the day's events. But these ruminations were so conflicting that I could not come to a balanced choice. I longed for a husband and children, yet I felt an overwhelming attraction to intimacy with God in prayer and meditation on Divine figures such as Christ and Mary. My time alone only exaggerated my opposing desires, causing confusion and loneliness in me. I could not make a choice for or against life as a nun. I kept hoping for a sign from God that would let me know which direction I should choose.

And then one day, on the Virginia Beach coastline, before the swelling Atlantic Ocean and an immense blue sky, with tears in my eyes, I cried in desperation to God, "Who am I?" I felt such a failure as a woman. I was lost with no identity of my own. But I heard from a voice within, "You are whomever I show you are!" I felt great peace in these words, feeling it was acceptable to feel unfinished and undefined, and that life would reveal who I was called to become. I chose to rejoin the nuns but at Caritas House in Portsmouth. I put aside my inner confusion and longing for a husband.

Caritas House was the name of the home the nuns moved to when Hosanna House closed. I do not know why Hosanna House closed but Caritas House was the location that some of the nuns moved to when it did close. Caritas House had been a rectory for priests in a church parish located in Portsmouth. The priests had vacated it and the Sisters for Christian Community took up residence shortly afterward. It was a place where three young women searched out the heart of the decision to become nuns with a lifestyle of charity, hence the name Caritas. There were two other young women now who also wanted to become nuns. In this home, with a committed nun as our guide, Karen, Glenda and I learned the lifestyle of a nun. We spent early mornings and late evenings in prayer and reflection. We worked among the poor at a thrift store and visited the elderly in their homes and in nursing homes. We asked ourselves questions. *Can I do this for all of my life without children and family of my own? Am I really being called by God to say no to married life and children? Does God really want ME? What talents do I bring to this lifestyle? Do I enjoy this lifestyle?*

The Sisters for Christian Community seemed to be the best avenue for me to become a contemplative. A contemplative is a special calling for a nun to a lifestyle totally centered on prayer, sort of cloistered with no ministry to others except for prayer for the world and its needs. I felt very attracted to this lifestyle but did not want to lock myself away from the world in a cloistered convent. The SFCC were committed to prayer and service. I felt so connected to God during my relationship with them. I admired their individuality, courage, loving and creative natures. Unconsciously, I was adopting their identities as my own, and I felt comfortable with this role. Something deep within me identified with them. It was as though an imprinting took place within my unconscious.

On a regular basis, all the Sisters for Christian Community from neighboring towns would get together for a meal, a barbeque or an evening out at a restaurant. Joyful sharing about each one's adventures and challenges marked these times. I saw all of them as women on the cusp of the changing roles of women in society. I admired the strength they had in leaving traditional orders to found this new order of nuns marked by freedom, challenge and responsiveness to the times in which they lived.

I carried this relationship with the nuns as the focal point of my life for many years to follow. I was particularly attracted to the mysterious ways in which they were powerful and influential, yet such insignificant and gentle women. They were not in positions of authority like my father had been or the priests whose roles put them in positions of power. These women had power through their personalities but they led others only as they chose to follow. They did not exert authority over others and viewed all people as peers. Many people consulted them for decisions about church and family life. We were close friends and grew as individuals and as a group. They were strong, yet seemed to need and enjoy me. For this I was grateful and grew in my own gentleness and confidence as a woman and as a nun.

While at Caritas House, the two other young women, Karen and Glenda, chose to leave the Sisters for Christian Community and join more traditional orders with a more structured lifestyle, and with specific rules for living out the vows. I am not aware of how they came to their decisions. I liked the freedom and independence that this order of nuns embodied in their philosophy of religious life. They believed that as women we should be responsible independently for our financial needs. They also encouraged each nun to identify and develop her own gifts and talents to be used in the service of God. They particularly felt a nun should not be dependant on the order itself for these parts of her life. After three years, I chose to make first vows with this order in 1975. First vows are the first step towards a permanent commitment to this way of life.

I moved with the nuns from Caritas House to a small town on the Eastern Shore of Virginia called Jamesville, to begin a ministry of presence among a rural people. We hoped to accomplish no more than a contemplative, rural life that spoke of peace and hospitality to the people of the Eastern Shore. As preparation for this move to a rural contemplative lifestyle, one of the nuns and I attended an Ira Progoff Dialogue House workshop on an intensive journal keeping method that incorporated Jungian principles. There was at this time a strong interest among religious men and women to bring psychology and spirituality and religious dogma together. This particular nun, Monica, had this interest and found out about the workshop. She had a masters degree in the field of psychology. First and foremost this workshop taught me to use active imagination in meditating. Active imagination is a meditation process described by Jung in which a person engages an image from a dream or fantasy or personal history. In this meditative exercise, one employs functions other than rational thought, such as painting, dance, yoga, transcendental meditation, prayer, or other meditative practice, which allows images and imagination to develop spontaneously. The purpose of this practice is to engage the image subject so that it unfolds its meaning, purpose, or message. It is a way of opening up the unconscious to one's consciousness. I adopted this process as a major part of my quiet private reflective periods I did every morning. I would rise early before the nuns met for prayer and journal about my life. I logged in this journal events from the day before, my feelings and thoughts, my hopes for the future, and memories of important people and events from my past. This is when I began meditating and connecting with my maternal grandmother, Granny Lodie. Thinking and writing about her encouraged me to embrace a life with simplicity and generosity. I used this journal and active imagining as the basis of all my personal reflections.

We moved to the Eastern Shore of Virginia in 1977 after this Dialogue House workshop. We crossed the 17-mile bay-bridge tunnel that span's the mouth of the Chesapeake Bay where it opens to the Atlantic Ocean. This bridge-tunnel connects the small rural area that is under the territory of Virginia but not connected to it by land. The section of Virginia comes just before you enter Maryland and Delaware. It is also known as the Delmarva Peninsula and is a strip of land surrounded on three sides by water, the Chesapeake Bay and the Atlantic Ocean. It extends between Delaware, Maryland and Virginia. It was in this isolated land that we established our search for a home to be our place for a rural life, lived off the resources of gardening, including the gleaning of the farm fields that covered this area. When harvesting of the crops was completed, we were allowed to gather up the leftovers. We wanted mostly to be prayerful women who supported themselves and served the community of people that lived there. Our ministry was one of prayer, presence, and service.

We established a rural home we called Mamre House on these principles. The name Mamre was chosen because it represented the story in the Bible where Abraham welcomed angels disguised as men, the real gift of hospitality. One of Abraham's particular views for following God was to welcome others, especially strangers with hospitality. This was his mark on faith. He believed God himself visited in these strangers and through gestures of hospitality. It was under the Oak of Mamre where he hosted three strangers who turned out to be angels. They brought Abraham the message that his wife, Sarah, would have a son in the next year. This was a miraculous message as Abraham and Sarah were beyond childbearing years. We hoped, in our struggle to build a new home and lifestyle, that God would visit us in the strangers we met. We believed these strangers and our hospitality would bring us fulfillment of hopes and fruitfulness.

We bought an old farmhouse and remodeled it. It was dilapidated to the point that it had broken windows and spider webs in the bare wall rooms and attic. We spent months searching for this farmhouse and acreage for our gardening. Even more months were involved in renovating the house into a home. We worked in the community as social workers and nurses. Each day we focused on gaining the trust of these isolated, rural people.

We welcomed the questions from our visitors about our lifestyle and hosted their visits to our home with simple gestures of hospitality. We offered food and drink to the men who helped us renovate the house. We got to know their wives and our neighbors on either side. Morning and evening prayers were centered on the needs of these people as they revealed their personal issues to us. There was a man without work, who worried about his family for whom he was the only provider; a woman who was abused by her husband and did not know how to handle her desires to be a good mother; small farmers and fishermen who struggled to survive among big corporate farming and seafood industries in the area. All were welcomed around our kitchen table, and over coffee or a meal, we listened to their stories of life and hardship.

I was doing well, for the most part with little question of my identity until I made an eight-day retreat with an insightful Jesuit priest, named George, as director. The retreat was held in a rural area of Maryland. Here I found a call from and for myself to creativity and self-expression, though I had no idea what that meant. Some deep dimension of myself was trying to connect me to the mission and purpose of my unique life. I knew that some undeveloped, creative, gifted part of myself was longing to be expressed. I just didn't know the how or what of this gift. I ached to be unique. George reflected back to me that I was unique and gifted though not well developed yet as a mature religious woman.

After the retreat, I returned to Mamre House ministry with a sense of distance and disconnect to its mission, feeling I somehow was being called to change my focus. Working as a nurse, I was the sole breadwinner for the Mamre House mission. Before the other nuns got well paying jobs, they depended on my income to pay the bills. In its beginning stages, I found a job easily. My salary was needed for the purchase of our home. After the retreat, I felt the need to focus more on the development of unique gifts and talents rather than the commitment of building a home. The others all had unique gifts such as creative sewing and home-making skills. One of the nuns eventually found part-time work as a social worker. She did grant writing for new projects. I thought she was particularly talented.

My skills as a nurse seemed routine, forced and lacking in creativity. I wanted to learn to express personal talents for the sake of serving God with purpose and intention. The nuns were frightened by my change of focus, fearing my desire to withdraw my financial support of Mamre House.

The nuns' immediate distrust of my new direction challenged me to stay on track with our shared commitment to the people of this rural area. I felt their lack of support of an essential call to individuality. It hurt deeply. I loved my home and the expression of myself as a nun. Leaving Mamre House did not enter my mind. There was no other life for me. I felt I had to accept that I was turning from responsibility if I even considered altering my roles as nurse and nun.

I lost contact with the Jesuit priest from the retreat and felt this as a profound rejection. In the eight days I was with him on the retreat, he became a positive father figure who believed in my potential. George was the first male figure in my life who mirrored that I had gifts and talents. He did this mirroring by asking me questions about how I saw my future developing. He encouraged me to discover and develop my unique gifts and talents. I was moved by his belief in me. Though I could have been a little 'hypomanic' during this retreat, it only felt like the excitement of being loved and affirmed by someone I admired. **Hypomania** is a state of excitement that is not out of control or marked by the signs of the true mania in bi-polar depression. It is often the stage just before true mania develops. Mania often precedes depression.

I wrote George about my disappointment when returning to Mamre House and requested to meet with him regarding how I could identify and develop my personal skills within the mission I had on the Eastern Shore. He never responded. The mail could have been lost or misplaced. George was a very busy man as the director of a large retreat house. Whatever the reason for his lack of response, I felt it as a painful rejection and reminder of the unavailability of my own father as a loving supporter for my potential as a creative woman. The loss of George's influence and belief in me set the stage for a deep depression that was to follow. Throughout this period of settling into a new home and job, I had forgotten my father's aggressive nature and felt I had a normal childhood with a good father. But his lack of belief in my potential and my own lack of belief in myself was part of my make-up. When I met George I became aware of a hunger in me to believe in myself and to be expressive of that belief through creativity. This hunger for affirmation from my practical and logical side was profoundly deep. This hunger was like a dark abyss that I had never really appreciated as part of me. The loss of contact with George and the nuns' lack of affirmation of my search for uniqueness brought this dark abyss within me to the surface. I began at this point to develop a black, almost chaotic depression.

Chapter V: The Break

Much of the next year and half was spent working on refurbishing Mamre House and working as a nurse in the rural area. I worked for a local health department supervising health aids who assisted the homebound elderly with their personal hygiene. Riding the back roads I found many lonely elderly women who were near disability. The state program allowed nurse aids to go their home once or twice a week to help them with bathing, housecleaning, and some minor medical care. I visited them every 6 weeks to ensure care was top quality. Though I empathized with the conditions of these poor elderly, I found the work boring and lacking in challenge for my nursing training. This boredom led to much sleepiness in the morning and afternoon lulls in a workday. Work on Mamre House involved strenuous physical activity and often at the end of a day I was exhausted.

We had decided to heat our home with a wood furnace and had to chop our own wood. This meant going into nearby forests with the permission of the owners to fell small trees. We loaded the wood into our small size Datsun pick-up. Then we unloaded, split, and sorted it for the wood fireplace. We did this on a weekly basis. Early mornings, we woke to a cold house that did heat up quickly with the wood stove. We also spent a summer painting the house. Several men from the community assisted with the interior remodeling and then the building of two extra rooms.

We gleaned soybeans from local farmers after a field had been harvested and made fresh soy flour for baking. Soybeans were soaked and made into soy burgers. Our lifestyle kept us close to nature but led me to a physical tiredness I could not shake. Many mornings I woke with sadness along with the exhaustion that was not repaired with eight hours of sleep.

I continued to make use of my journal keeping, logging dreams from the nighttime, but did not know how to work with these dreams in any productive manner. I often dreamed of Richard, wishing I had not lost him or the future he had offered me in marriage. Sadness that related to loss of George's influence on my life also tormented me. I had thoughts of returning to school for a master's, hoping this would help me develop gifts and talents in a unique way. But I couldn't decide on what I would want to study. And the uniqueness I desired was still just a vague wish I could not describe.

Over the next two years, I buried my inner call to be uniquely creative and shape my destiny. I wanted to make sense of the awareness from the retreat with George of the unexpressed potential

69

within me, specifically to believe in myself through creative outlets. I felt lost in how to go about achieving this. Lack of direction and leadership plunged me into an inner search I could not deal with alone. Often in my morning and evening prayers, I stared out the window, wondering why I had become so lost and unfulfilled. Depression, marked by what seemed to me to be a lifetime of unfulfilled dreams, overwhelmed me. It seemed I had been sad and incomplete all my life.

In private prayer time, I began to see images of suffering, contorted faces in the bushes and trees outside my window. Voices and faces of people asking me to sooth their hurts filled my imagination and denied me sleep. These were not faces of anyone I knew, just people with sad or suffering facial expressions.

These images seemed to stare at me and say, "Why do I have to suffer so?" Why I or anyone had to experience suffering or sadness was a question I could not answer. I found concentration difficult. Only the poem by Heidi Neumark brought me comfort:

"How beautiful on the mountains are the feet of one who brings good news, feet that have been bruised and torn but kept on walking bare upon the groaning earth, without the comfort shoes afford. Harder than walking over seas, you walk with us. My heart shakes off her dull and withered leaves and becomes a burning bush before your feet."

I found this poem one day while reading a monthly magazine we got delivered to the house. It was called "Contemplative." I memorized this poem and recited it every morning. It expressed my desire to integrate and give reverence to my life journey at a time when I was unable to do this for myself. I prayed this poem every day as I gazed into the illusions of suffering faces I saw in nature's designs all around me. In this poem, I found without knowing it an expression of the suffering in my own life and my connection to the suffering of others.

In the midst of this two-year depression at Mamre House, my longing for an intimate connection to God never left me. Religious life allowed this longing a place for its expression; but fulfillment never came. I never knew peace for many years even with the eventual attempt at married life. I was drowning in an overwhelming undercurrent of the sea I was subconsciously exploring in depression. Depression brings us into a deep darkness where we face fears and wounds. This can be a healthy attempt by the psyche to heal itself. I tried to reason with this negative mood and the suffering faces my imagination conjured up. Through rational attempts with my thinking skills, I tried to answer the question of why I was experiencing this darkness. But despondency grew every day to cripple my functioning as a nurse and nun. I felt overwhelmed by the demands of nursing duties and the structure of morning and evening prayers. I had to drag myself out of bed every morning and sought sleep before sunset. Though I felt much love from the nuns, I never shared my depressive thoughts and imagination with them.

In 1979, two years after the first retreat, I made another eight-day retreat with a different priest-director. This retreat was held in Richmond, Virginia in an old two-story house that once was home to seminarians preparing for the priesthood. Now it had been turned into

71

a place where mostly nuns and priests went for private, quiet, meditative time. The director also offered eight-day retreats that were focused on meditating on a certain decision one had to make. The retreat was spent in eight days of silence with daily visits to the director for guidance in prayer regarding the situation one brought to the retreat for reflection. I was trying to decide when I should make final vows. I just could not peacefully say a wholehearted yes to it for a reason I could not name. I focused my prayers, while on this retreat, on my desire to be a nun, my lack of ability to live such a life with joy, and the possible reason for the depression that surrounded me. My childhood memories of neglect and abuse from my father's aggressive discipline surfaced as a major part of this retreat's reflections. I spent each day with four or five prayer and reflective periods, attended daily mass, and met with the director for an hour. Most of the time I could not share much of my reflection with the director except to say, "I am still unsure about what God wants from me." He would give me scripture to use as the basis of my prayer and reflection, but I often wandered off in thought rather than focus on these scriptures.

Around 7 p.m. on the 7th day of this eight day retreat, I encountered, in my imagination and prayers, racing thoughts and images. The images centered on a three-year-old child, dressed in a red dress, playing in a circus with a clown as they played on a swing set and merry-go-round. At first the images were fun and brought good feelings to me about my childhood. But soon the clown became mean and the merry-go-round spun out of control, throwing the child into the air. These images took on a life of their own, developing without my conscious control. In my out-of-control imagination, these images became ugly and aggressive towards each other with grotesque faces and gestures of attack. By this point, I had lost willful control of the images and the energy they contained.

I could not sleep. I was plagued by an imagination gone haywire. I lacked a leader or even a relationship in reality that could guide me out of this developing experience with bullish mania and the labyrinth of mental illness. My overly logical and thinking function was moving so fast and tangentially that I was beginning to experience the chaos of mania.

The runaway thinking and images broke through my conscious control and shouted, "Come Out!" calling me into a painfully bright light just beyond the door of my dark room. I feared the light intensely. This light was imagined to be the resurrected Christ and His demands that I become a saint. It was a call to come out from a dungeon like Lazarus was called out from the tomb. Then, in the dark of my room, I felt on my ear, a breath that whispered "Evil" in a taunting voice. I was shaken with fear. The dark room was like a tomb filled with evil spirits. The bright light of the demanding Christ-figure from beyond the door trapped me in motionless terror.

Terrified by these hallucinations and illusions, I ran from my room to the room of the priest directing the retreat. By now, it was about 2 a.m. I shared with him the journal I kept during these days of silence with extensive prayer and thinking. I am sure my journal sounded incoherent and he was able to see I was experiencing a break with reality. He advised that I stop all prayer and reflections. He invited me to just listen to music in his silent presence. He chose to play Pachelbel's *Canon,* which relaxed and calmed my fears so that by five a.m., I was able to return to my room. At his recommendation, I began preparations to go home and see a psychiatrist. It is mysterious and meaningful to me how powerful this music was as a healing force at this disturbing point in my life.

All eight days of the retreat were marked by an inability to sleep or control my imagination. I sat up all night with my mind stimulated with thought and wandering fantasies about where I had been in my life and why I existed. I did not attempt to even lie down in bed. I felt no need of sleep. This retreat experience could have had the power to heal my childhood memories, if I had developed an ego with balanced logic, emotions and values, or if someone with this balance could have engaged me. I have read of John Weir Perry's approach to psychosis where he attempted to understand the psychosis of his patients and see what the psyche was trying to achieve with the images. He believed psychosis was an attempt of the psyche to heal itself. The clown, whom I often played in my childhood home, the little girl in the red dress, the bright light of the masculine in the image of Christ, and the terrifying dark of the intuitive feminine in the tomb of my room, all represented parts of myself I needed to integrate. The integration of reasoning, instinct, intuition, and feelings was the challenge that faced me. It would take a lifetime to achieve this integration.

Three days passed from the time I left the retreat house to the time I was admitted to a mental hospital. I have tried remembering what went on during these three days, but I remember only bits and pieces.

How I got home to Mamre House or arriving at Mamre House is gone from my recollection. I don't remember any conversations about what had happened on the retreat or how I felt. It seems I engaged no one verbally and no one engaged me. I know I was unable to sleep for nine or ten days. Perhaps I appeared disturbed and kept the nuns at a distance. Whatever went on, I remember little of those days, but I have clear memory of some of what was going on inside me.

These days were filled with the feeling of an intense fire burning within me that cold showers could not calm. The circle of flames from my youth, when my father set a fire around me, now seemed ablaze within me. There was an inner excitement, like an adrenalin rush, only filled with fear along with the excitation. My body felt on fire. As I showered with cold water, begging God to put out the fire, I felt the call to greatness from the bright light of Christ, while an awesome warning of fear and evil, from the breath on my ear, triggered panic. I could not connect emotionally with the nuns as I waited for hospitalization. No one could reach or touch where I was mentally.

In my reflections now, it seems that this trembling fire within me hoped for One to channel its energy in a positive direction without attempting to bury it deep away from conscious reach. Somehow it was as though this fire was reaching out to me from my childhood, but my lack of courage and honed instinct kept me from directing its powerfully destructive capacity. There was no one who understood what I was going through, including myself. It seems I should have been able to reason with the negative memories from my life, but I was too overwhelmed by them and my youthful desire to be unique and great.

The nuns had arranged for me to see a favored psychiatrist of theirs, but before the appointment could take place, my father heard from the nuns of my incident with psychosis. He came, with my mother, in my older brother's private plane, to pick me up and place me in a hospital near our home in Louisiana. I do remember walking from an airplane hanger with my father who was carrying his doctor bag. We got onboard the small white jet during daylight. The trip took some hours as I remember seeing only night out of the airplane windows. I did not say a word on the entire trip home. Once in the hospital, extensive testing was done to determine that there was no physical cause for my brain malfunctions. Then the mental health staff began working with me. The hospital was in Lake Charles, a large town about thirty-five miles from my original home, in Louisiana.

My first experience of paranoia came to me in the hospital in Lake Charles where staff and my psychiatrist wanted only one thing from me: normal behaviors and thinking they described as acceptable in society. They wanted me to lose touch with this fire of masculine and feminine energy represented by the experience of the opposing images and voices from my psychotic event. It seemed to me that the staff wanted me to relate only to concrete reality in a superficial manner. Any talk of this fire from within me led to increases in medication and limitations of my freedom through the increased medication. I learned to distrust the staff, hide my fire, and fake a willfully controlled approach to life. I did not ask questions about anything they wanted me to do. The hospital routine of three meals a day, sessions with the doctor and quiet time was followed without any indication of my dissatisfaction. In my quiet time, I simply prayed the rosary to pass the time. They would make rounds in the night, and I always pretended to be asleep so they would not be aware of my insomnia. I focused on pleasing them.

I chose to show only my functioning personality so that I could get out of the jail they chose for me. I returned as quickly as possible to my pre-psychotic functioning since this is what the hospital seemed to want from me. I obeyed all the rules and was purposely cordial and polite. Please and thank you was part of my daily interactions with staff, along with agreeable participation in all activities. I gave up speaking to the doctor of my desires to understand the psychotic event and its profound energy.

This is not to say that the hospital's safe, protective environment and the medication regimen were not good for me. However, the lack of art therapy and a spiritual approach to the psychic wound I was dealing with and needed to talk about, served to extend the healing process to years longer than it might have required. I believe, after reading John Weir Perry's book, *Far Side of Madness*, that my pre-psychotic state of depression as a nurse and nun was more ill than the actual event with psychosis. The spontaneous images from my unconscious were trying desperately, symbolically, to right the wrong that had been done in my life. The wrongful behavior, which I had endured as a child and young adult, was the cause of my depression. I needed to confront and assimilate these attacks, which were the real and psychological rape experiences from my previous years, rather than ignore them. Talking about the hallucinations and illusions from the retreat was a way of connecting me to these difficult memories. The intrusive bright light of Christ and the terrifying evil voice were expressions of my broken psyche, broken by the two violating experiences I had earlier in my life. Though talking about these hallucinations made me tremble, I needed to make sense of them. They seemed very important to my psychological development.

This challenge from the good and evil, light and dark images, was the beginning of my bi-polar experience with mental illness. It was the beginning of the healing of a profound split in the wounded masculine-logic and feminine-feeling dimensions of my psyche. This incident with psychosis began the transition to the third phase of my life, which was marked by bipolar mental illness and its ravages on my life.

I was discharged after three weeks from the hospital to my parents' home in Jennings, Louisiana. Here, I followed their directions and took my medication until I could return to my home in Virginia. My parents told me when to get out of bed, when to eat, and when I could be alone. They observed my daily routine including the taking of medication. There were no in depth discussions on how I felt inside. I slept well and did not wander much in thought. But I felt very bored and trapped. I longed to return to the nuns in Virginia.

In looking back on this experience with psychosis and mania, it seems that, for me, mental illness was basically learning to deal with profound opposites. I express this mostly as the difference between the masculine and feminine aspects of one's soul. Like the sun that is a glaring, scorching, powerful light, masculine logic can leave no room for reflection and mystery. Everything is stark, clear, and demanding in its forcefulness. My father was like the sun, powerful and demanding. I connected this experience of my father to the image of the bright light of Christ. As a child, I knew my father was wrong many times, such as when he surrounded me with fire to teach me a lesson. Sometimes people use logic to prove the validity of some fact. Logic does not take into account the whole picture of a situation and can be valid but not the truth. Logic does not equal right. I translated the fear of my father into feelings of fear and mistrust of icons of Christ, powerful and not to be trusted. I become unsure of my relationship with Christ whom I had always felt attracted to and with whom I desired a close relationship.

The opposite of the sun is the light of the moon. With this light one is reflective and sees shadows with deeper dimensions. There is no room for logic in this light. I see this as a feminine approach to thinking, based more on feelings and intuition, full of mystery with varying interpretations of reality, compassionate in understanding, yet capable of frightening awareness. The tomb-like dark of my room and the taunting breath on my ear seemed to emerge from my lack of skill in handling emotions and intuitions. I was not able to assimilate a feminine approach to reasoning.

I had to learn through mental illness, which approach, the bright light of the sun or the reflective light of the moon, was most natural for me. I was not skilled in thinking rationally or in using my intuition as a guide in decision-making. It takes both skills to make a good choice in anything but I had neither skill very well developed. At the time of my psychotic experience, I was confronted with these opposites in powerful symbols of evil voices and a bright light. The feminine approach with intuition was dark, chaotic and undefined while the masculine approach with rational thinking was too stark and demanding. The masculine and feminine dimensions of my own soul were battling each other. It would be years before this battle would resolve as the creative co-existence of the two.

Third phase of my life: Part I
The Dying of Self Identity Roles

Chapter VI: Living alone as a Nun

In the later part of 1979, I was out of the hospital and on medication. I functioned well enough to return to Virginia and Mamre House with the nuns. There, I toyed for two more years with the decision to make final vows. Mental illness was diagnosed, and I knew I carried a special identity and label that was cherished by none, especially not by me. When my psychiatrist first told me I had a major affective disorder known as manic-depressive mental illness, I was relieved that there was something I could point to as the cause of my feelings of failure. I could find no pride in being a college graduate, a Navy officer, or a Catholic nun. At least now, there was something I could blame for this lack of self-worth. Medications had stopped the runaway thinking and hallucinations, but depressive thoughts and an inability to just get out of bed took all hope from me. Around eleven a.m. most mornings, the nuns would come and insist I get up and begin my day's activities. I could see no cure for my inadequacies as a person.

It was as though the unique, undefined dimension of myself that had longed to be expressed had emerged; it was ugly. I had longed all my life to be a special person that stood out from the rest. Now I stood out from others but in a way that stigmatized me rather than praised me. My diagnosis of mental illness was something I was ashamed of and it exaggerated my feelings of poor self-worth.

During this phase of returning to Mamre House with a diagnosis of mental illness, I was challenged by the tasks of learning to handle my bipolar nature of highs and lows, and at the same time, make a decision about final vows. It was like a dungeon of darkness in which I was trapped by isolated, desperate searching.

The Sisters for Christian Community were not challenging me to make final vows; I felt, after ten years as a nun, I should be able to answer that this was for life. I just could not answer that question in my heart. I knew I could not make it on my own without a structured life to give me a sense of home and belonging, yet something from within was pulling me and preventing me from wholeheartedly living the life of a nun, the only real lifestyle I had ever known. Two years of struggling with depression and failed attempts to be a contributing part of the home life with the nuns left me with the only choice I could see, to leave Mamre House. Dragging myself to morning and evening prayer, poor participation in household chores like cooking and cleaning, and going to bed early all contributed to my feelings of unworthiness for the ministry of Mamre House.

Leaving Mamre House meant leaving the only genuine love of my life: the nuns and our shared missionary lifestyle. But I resented and rebelled against their vision of religious life and I could not identify why. I just could not find a way to develop and express my uniqueness as a nun. I had no creative outlets. Once in an attempt to be unique and creative, I came home with new, colored, floral-print sheets and comforter for my bed. This angered one of the nuns who saw me as self-centered. She and I verbally attacked each other for these differing views of how I should choose to be a part of the Mamre lifestyle. She felt deeply the absence of my contributions to our home life and she had no idea of the depth of my inadequacies in daily functioning. She knew of my mental illness but did not seem to understand the broadness of its impact on all my behaviors. She only saw my lack of contribution to daily life.

So in 1982, I chose to take my torn, emotionally unstable personality away from the peaceful mission of Mamre House. I chose to move to find an avenue to personal peace and happiness as a nun somewhere else. I felt that I was destroying the calm, creative atmosphere of Mamre House with my needs to be unique and my depression. I left to relieve them of my presence. I put aside my questioning of religious life and made an impulsive decision to say yes to life as a nun. I made final vows in 1982, packed up, and courageously moved alone to begin a search for new life.

While making final vows at a retreat house in Richmond, Virginia,

I met a couple that lived in Charlottesville, Virginia. I shared with them my plans to move and begin a new life somewhere. They invited me to Charlottesville, offering me their basement apartment as my living space to get started on this new leg of my journey. Once there, I began working in two part-time jobs as a nurse, one in a hospice and the other in a psychiatric hospital. This work provided me an income and focus for my daily living.

As a hospice nurse, I cared for one woman in particular who was about my age. She was dying at home with her husband and two adopted children to surround her. When death came one night around midnight, I was there. The husband had called me. Sue, his wife, developed a new pain he could not relieve with the current medication. After I examined her and discussed her case with the hospice doctor, a new pain med was prescribed. Sue began to rest comfortably. As I began packing up to leave, Sue suddenly gripped with a choking episode. Sue's husband panicked. I coached him to calm and comfort her with his loving embrace. She relaxed again and her last breath was for the words she had spoken often in her life, "I love you." They were both prepared for this separation because of several years of struggling with advancing cancer. I felt honored to be a part of their journey. It seems I had found the real reason I had become a nurse, which was to assist the dying and their families. Later in life, I developed the awareness that my primary role as a nurse was to help suffering people in grave transitions in life, to offer compassion at the crossroads in life.

Because there was not sufficient income with this hospice job, I had to supplement my finances with another nursing position.

In the psychiatric hospital, my primary role was medication nurse. I was distant and fearful of my patients. I think the main reason for this fear was over-identification with them. I saw myself in their stories and behaviors. I suppose I empathized too much and chose distance to protect them and myself.

After about 7 months of working these two jobs, I felt strong enough, mentally and financially, to move out of the basement apartment to follow a dream. I felt drawn to live a simple rustic life in the Blue Ridge Mountains that surrounded Charlottesville.

I would like to note here that my decision making skills were poor, probably a symptom of my illness itself. There were many periods of my life when I gave less than a year to the task of attempting to make the situations I had chosen work out. But often, I became bored or frustrated with the demands of daily life. Part of my mental illness was the inability to connect with reality as it is and accept the requirements it takes to make it work. Soon after a choice of job or living situation, I sought some new lifestyle without giving the present one enough time and effort. I had worked in Charlottesville for about 7 months when I chose to leave both jobs and my basement apartment to move to the mountains.

The decision to live in the mountains came because of the solitude and peace I experienced when visiting the beautiful mountain terrain. It called me to a life of isolation and prayer. I found a trailer for rent in the mountains with my nearest neighbor five miles away. I moved in and set up home. My trailer was small, but I made one room into a bedroom and the other into a prayer room. The kitchenette was sufficient for one person. I started work as a nurse at a local health department, providing nursing supervision to homebound elderly in this rural county.

This new beginning was happy and hopeful. I enjoyed the hills and mountaintop views. Sitting beside the babbling creek near my home gave me great peace. But this did not last for long.

My attempts to develop the sense I had of religious life in solitude and service were constantly interrupted by racing, intense inner energy and unstable emotional eruptions from the mental illness I carried within the crevices of my soul. As I walked through the forests of the Blue Ridge Mountains, voices frequently taunted me and I felt I had to choose between a structured, successful life as a nurse and a tumultuous underground struggle between the masculine and feminine images in my dreams and fantasies. These tensions led to paranoia and distrust of others in my work as a nurse and in socializing with friends.

My dreams and fantasies were marked by conflict between images of men and women and even sometimes fantasies of subversive plots with government agencies. On one occasion, the voices consisted of a man and woman speaking from a television interview about their undercover work with the CIA. I realized there was no television within earshot. These voices caused me great fear and I called my psychiatrist, hoping for a medication adjustment. He encouraged me to realize these were benign hallucinations, benign because I recognized them as invalid and had reached out for help. Had I not had the insight that these voices were **projections** from my unconscious, I could have become very tangled in a web of unrealistic perceptions. I suppose my nursing background enabled me to have this insight. The voices did not stop, but I knew I should not listen to or obey them.

At work, I performed my duties well enough, but side effects from medication caused my hands to tremble and my voice to quiver. I knew I lacked a pleasing professional persona. Other staff members such as my supervising nurse were expressive of compassion for clients while still being organized and decisive about how to handle the many work demands in a day. I, on the other hand, chose not to discuss any aspects of my work with anyone. My hands trembled as I shuffled papers on my desk to give to my supervisor. My handwriting was illegible due to the tremors. I stumbled over words as I tried to defend my writing skills. I did not want to tell anyone I was bi-polar or that I took medication. I feared their rejection and judgment because of the stigma of mental illness. I often heard jokes about the *crazy* people in the world, and if they were not laughed at, they were then pitied or feared. I stayed away from friendships, fearing I would have to explain my tremors.

I could feel myself losing grip with reality, not knowing whom I could trust with my unstable inner identity. I shared with no one my personal or professional struggles. My psychiatrist was too far away for regular encounters. My associations at work were no more than work partners. I was not close enough to the two friends I had developed. One was another nurse at work who seemed interested in my role as a nun and asked questions about it. She wondered what it was like for a nun to live alone in the mountains and if the Church approved of such a lifestyle. The other was a woman from church who had several children. I saw her seldom. I could not tell anyone of my inner mental state with its tensions and fears.

After eight months of living alone in solitude on this beautiful mountain ridge, I realized that my mental illness was beyond my self-control. Hearing voices, lack of sleep, and tears of loneliness drove me to return to Louisiana just to be near people who kept calling me to come home, my original family. It seemed to me, at the time, the only option I had to protect me from an incapacitating madness. Fear drove me to say yes to their invitations. They were the only people in my life that offered the hope of grounding me in reality without denying my inner struggle. They knew I was ill and yet wanted me to come home to them. In 1984, after 15 months in the Charlottesville area, I moved back to Louisiana.

At first, the connection to work as a hospice nurse in Lafayette, Louisiana was rich, challenging, and felt right for me. The presence of my large family was outside my awareness because of the boundary I set up for the sake of self-protection. I never shared my inner struggles with my parents or siblings. I always felt uncomfortable with the family as a group. It seemed it was too large and dynamic for my shy nature to endure for very long. On an individual basis, my encounters with them were loving and supportive, but they all had spouses and children of their own. I knew I was outside of those commitments.

I lived alone in Carencro, Louisiana with my sister and her family and my parents as next-door neighbors on either side of me. Carencro was a small rural town near Lafayette. I worked for a newly developed hospice program in the heart of Acadiana, among the Cajun people. Acadiana is a widespread area in southwest Louisiana, near Baton Rouge. Its center is Lafayette. It is marked by the Cajun lifestyle of simplicity, family, ritual and festival. There were many routine family activities such as ten a.m. and two p.m. coffee breaks, even with strangers. Hunting and fishing activities were enjoyed in everyone's lifestyles. Bayou living and its close connection to nature were familiar to all.

Intense feelings of love and hope for these people I served were a part of my morning and evening prayer times, but I just could not find a way to fully express that love. In my self-created isolation, I yearned for an intimate connection with another. Still, I made no intimate contacts. I chose not to share myself with anyone so I never had a relationship that was mutually loving. The only relationships I had were through my nursing; and patients offered me only a one-way relationship in which I listened to their stories of life.

I believed that God knew how unsuccessful I felt as a nurse and nun. My faith in God's mercy kept me striving to become better in these roles, never realizing what I really needed was to open up to a friend who believed in me. I did not know how to break out of the roles I had chosen, in order to encounter another person on an intimate level. My sense of God's love for others and me was strong, but I felt so uncomfortable reaching out to others. Lack of an emotional connection to others left me feeling unfinished and incomplete. I would attach to clients who were in hospice but when they died, I was left alone again, lacking involvement with others. There had to be more to life than dying. I did not realize that I was using my roles to validate myself as valuable rather than as an avenue of expressing an inherent worthiness I knew to be true.

During this phase of my life, I was also strongly at odds with my father and the side of him that ridiculed the fragile aspects of life. I felt compassion for the poor who were discriminated and marginalized in society. I felt angry at society and the government for this imbalance of wealth and opportunity. My father was angered by my views. We experienced this division in the contrasting values we held politically, religiously and socially. He and I argued frequently; always I left feeling crushed in spirit. As a Republican, he held strong views of the importance of financial independence for all individuals. As a Democrat, I saw the importance of society and government in assisting with the financial needs of the poor and disadvantaged.

These political arguments led to even physical violence between us. Once I called the police as he tried to restrain me in his anger over my views. He left before the police arrived. The police offered me the only option they could see for my struggles with my father and that was to get a restraining order to keep us apart. I tried to avoid him, but the bull in me and his own bullish nature attracted and repelled each other constantly. My angry assertions never resulted in him showing compassion towards my nature or views on life.

Daddy believed the sole cause of my mental health problems was due to one physiological reason. He knew that the biochemical imbalances in my brain would respond to medication. He did not see any value in exploring the environmental or relationship factors that contributed to my unhappiness. Daddy believed that every time I had a mood swing it was because I had gone off my medication. I was very faithful to my medication regimen, knowing I did not want to return to the frightening psychosis I had experienced while on retreat. I could not convince Daddy that my mental illness had more than biochemical causes. As far as I know, he never accepted any responsibility as a contributor to my state of affairs.

Finally, in a desperate measure to stop these painful encounters with him and after the physical altercation mentioned above, I got a restraining order against him. Since my parents were the only people in my life who I visited on a regular basis, I often cried tears of loneliness during this separation. I broke the order after three months, not being able to bear the separation from my parents. I still loved and needed them regardless of fighting with my father. In the three months of legal distance between us, I realized that running from those whom I loved or hated was not the answer to my unhappiness. The mystery of forgiveness entered my thoughts during this time apart. I learned to forgive myself for not being the daughter I had hoped to be and I forgave my parents for not being the parents I hoped to have.

The day I returned to visiting my parents against the restraining order was marked mostly by silence. We cried together, but did not talk about what divided us. We shared coffee and spoke of the weather. My mother, with tears in her eyes, asked, "Why did you get that restraining order?" With an equally tearful state, I motioned for silence by gently putting my hand to my mouth, and said, "Please, Mom, let's not go there." We made an unspoken pact to never talk about what divided us. Respect for each other as unique persons became a part of our manner of relating. We never grew any closer in intimacy but never argued again either.

Chapter VII: First Marriage

In 1985, after six months of living alone and working as a hospice nurse in Louisiana, my first husband entered my life. James was a medical doctor for the hospice program where I worked. He was very successful as a physician. He had a scientific mind, yet compassionate heart and hands. This attracted me intensely and, surprisingly to me, sexually.

One night we made a 2 a.m. house call to one of our dying patients. I watched as James examined this woman to discover what was causing her pain. He caringly interviewed her for her emotional and physical problems of the last few days. Doing a physical assessment, he gently pressed her abdomen and palpated her tenderness. Skillfully diagnosing the advancing cancer's invasion of nearby organs and nerve endings, he administered the medicine that quickly relieved the client's pain. I was deeply moved and sexually stimulated watching his tenderness and skill.

That night when I went to bed, I dreamed my cat was showing James her attraction and approval of him by rubbing against his legs and kneading his flesh with her paws on his back. I woke stunned with how powerfully attracted I was to this man.

Later that day, James and I shared our assessment of the client from the night before. We talked about her and her family's stressors in the face of death. In this discussion I learned of his fragile and vulnerable feelings towards death. Caring for the dying had not relieved his fears of death. I expressed admiration of him because of his skill and compassionate approach to the dying. I even shared my feelings of fondness for him, saying, "I could easily be in love with you." He responded by opening himself and his life to me.

James was a widower and was overwhelmed that someone found him attractive. He was used to fame as a successful doctor. But with the death of his wife, he had experienced significant loneliness. James invited me to meet his family, including his children who were about my age. The fact that he was thirty years my senior seemed unimportant in the whole decision making process of saying "yes" to his invitation of marriage. Though I felt frightened of this new relationship, marriage was a dream I had always held close to my heart but thought was outside my reach. Marriage was a symbol of union and home, something I needed. I left the Sisters for Christian Community without much thought. James and I never even went on a date. We went straight from being work partners to being lovers. James expressed a desire to marry immediately after I told him I could easily be in love with him. I felt enamored by his attraction to me.

Somehow James, in his aged wisdom, never saw the immature woman I was at the time. He admired and needed me, and saw nothing but the loving, generous, compassionate professional persona I carried as a hospice nurse. By this time, most of the tremors had stopped and I functioned well as a nurse. James knew, from discussions with my father at medical society meetings, of my mental illness. Yet, in the six months we worked together, James had only experienced me as a successfully functioning nurse and nun. He was in love with the roles I chose rather than the real me that no one saw. I married James one month after sharing my attraction to him. We both rushed headlong into this union.

The decision to marry was one of my happy, impulsive choices made during a period of exhilaration and hypomania. James and I married one Saturday afternoon, with a small family gathering in his backyard. The yard was filled with flowers and joy. Everyone seemed to be happy for both James and me.

Marriage to James was a special stepping-stone in my life. I moved out of the trap of being alone as a nun and into a common life with others I so longed to know. Now, instead of being alone at social and family gatherings, I had a partner. At the time, we felt good together as a couple.

We chose not to have children. I feared passing my illness on genetically to a child. I feared not being a good mother due to my illness. My medication at the time, lithium, would also have been harmful to a fetus. I remember going for long walks in the neighborhood, imagining what pleasure I would get from holding an infant in my arms. But then my mind would quickly see how my terrible depressive periods would block me from meeting this tiny person's needs for survival. I had known of depressed mothers and their 'failure to thrive' babies through my nursing experience. I knew I could not take on the responsibility of a child.

After four years of marriage, I began to discover a feeling that my marriage was dull and empty. James was a disciplined exerciser, writer, and doctor. He spent his day busy with routine involvement with these activities. James was more comfortable with the image of himself as the provider and had asked me to leave nursing. I did stop working for the hospice program and began looking for something else to do with my time. My lack of personal interests or skills left me bored and isolated from James and his busy days.

At his encouragement, I tried to fill my time working as an artist. I loved the feel of my hands shaping things with the clay. I developed this interest just by watching a sculptor one day as she created an image of a Madonna and Child. I began playing with clay and did create some beautiful representations of my inner traits of compassion and devotion to God that had been a part my personality for many years. I was a compassionate, prayerful, reflective woman even in the midst of depression. Later in my life, I realized these representations of my personality traits were creative feminine figures from my nighttime dreams and imagination, which allowed an undeveloped, nurturing energy to emerge. I fashioned these images into clay sculptures.

Three sculptures in particular stand out for me. One was an image of a youthful feminine figure, her body twisted up from a kneeling position, carrying something heavy wrapped in her arms, yet reaching up to God with joy on her face. The second was of a young, pregnant woman with an unusually beautiful expression of joy in her smile. The third was of a strong man kneeling, in compassion, to lift a dying man from his bed.

I have come to see these images as representing parts of my unconscious that believed in my journey. As the sculptures revealed, I was a woman carrying a burden but with my eyes toward God and His mercy. I was, in the darkness of my depression, like a pregnant woman with hidden new life within her. And like the sculpture of the strong man lifting the dying, I was reaching out to others with burdens. At the time of their creation, I only viewed them as art to be critiqued or sold for an income. I did not have an art teacher and never felt confident enough about my creations to take them for formal evaluation. I had no teacher for this new realm of self-expression and felt myself to be a failure at it. My own logical, critical evaluation of my artistic skills soon buried this creative, feminine energy. I gave up working as an artist.

Intense longing for self-expression, coupled with periods of depression and mania, plagued my married life, eventually leading to divorce. In manic episodes, I would stay up late and work in my studio with the clay. James would have to ask me to come to bed. Other times, hospitalizations because of a desire for suicide were common. I kept a bottle of whisky and a rope hidden in the garage as my plan for suicide. I believed a little alcohol intoxication would make hanging myself easier by encouraging impulsiveness. In the hospital, I could talk about these suicide wishes that I never told James about. Sometimes I could connect the depression directly to the lack of children. Other times, the depression had no rational explanation or connection to any event. Numerous medication adjustments were done in the hospital. I tried several different types of antidepressants and each worked for only a short period. I had gained much weight as side effects of these medications and lay in a chair much of the day. I tried keeping a journal as I had done in my earlier life but just couldn't maintain the discipline of writing everyday. James knew this was not the way the woman he admired coped with life before we were married. He hoped a psychiatrist would bring me back to my earlier successful image as a nurse. James never struggled with emotions himself and did not seem to empathize with my emotional expressions of sadness. He saw me as an artist with potential and could not understand why I was not intent on this new direction. He saw my depressive mood as an illness to be treated rather than feelings to be valued.

In contrast to James, I felt depressive feelings usually come from somewhere and are often connected to something. My biochemical imbalance exaggerated my feelings of sadness, but the feelings themselves needed to be understood, valued, and connected to real facets of my life. James and my psychiatrist in Louisiana only saw mood swings that needed treatment with medication adjustments. I was deeply saddened by the reality that I could not be a mother. I missed nursing and the discipline of going to work every day. This structured type of day had held my depressive tendencies at bay for many years. Now without the responsibility of needing to earn a living, I sank into despair.

Hospitalization was the major way James and I dealt with this despair. The medical staff and my psychiatrist all approached me with the science of medication to cure all my unhappiness. It never worked well. Numerous medication adjustments were done, but no sustained improvement in my sadness ever developed. The jagged edges of my manic-depressive nature soon began to disable my commitment to James. Particularly depression, which caused me to withdraw totally from him, became a wedge between us.

Around the spring of 1985, I sought out Jungian therapy on my own. I had heard of a new therapist in town, who had a Jungian approach and I was attracted to this style of treatment. Here begins my real story of improvement.

Chapter VIII: Beginning of Jungian Therapy

I must comment on the golden thread that has been woven throughout my journey so far, a Jungian approach to life. As I said earlier, in 1975 before moving to the Eastern Shore, I attended an Ira Progoff Dialogue House workshop on journal keeping and self-discovery. This workshop involved several days of learning meditation and journal keeping. The journal was a notebook with several sections devoted to many different areas of one's life such as memories, dreams, fantasies and aspirations. Imaginative dialoging with the characters written in this journal was part of the process of the journal keeping. This dialogue involved allowing a character from your imagination to speak to you while you wrote what that character said. You then responded to the character in your writing also. This allowed a person to expand and develop all these facets of soul and personality.

All my adult life, journaling, active imagination, and awareness of fantasies have marked my way of living and self-expression. These were avenues for growth that seemed so vivid and fruitful to me. I always used them out of a desire for adoration of God and discovery of Self. This was the backbone of my prayer life and journal keeping as a nun. Through journal keeping, I hoped to grow closer to God and develop better understanding of my Self and my unique talents.

The word Self is used as a Jungian concept. Jane Hollister Wheelwright in her book, *For Women Growing Older: The Animus,* gave a definition of the Self that was clearest for me. It is the main facet of the psyche and the archetype of wholeness that transcends the individual's ego. Knowing the true Self and allowing it to be forefront in one's life is the ultimate purpose of a journey to individuation. Ms. Wheelwright states that individuation involves living a life in relation to the Self and in relationship with others, and includes expressing one's strengths and weaknesses.

Using the Progoff-style of journaling, I struggled to live in connection to God and discover more about my Self, but I was failing due to my mental illness and my lack of ability to handle the material written in my daily journal. In manic periods, my journal contained thoughts gone haywire with wandering and tangential thinking that never made sense to me the next day. In depression I focused on sad events but couldn't be faithful to the journal keeping process. My reflections on memories, dreams and aspirations always spiraled down into depression and I gave up on journaling. I was trying to apply Jungian principles of encountering the subconscious without the help of a guide or therapist. Journaling and meditating on what I wrote led me into greater confusion or depression.

While married to James, I felt I had exhausted all the help I was going to get from medication and psychiatry. Several hospitalizations for depression had only resulted in a feeling of despair. Repeated attempts to find the right medication to control my mania and depression were not successful. Antidepressants work in many different ways and my doctor searched for the medication that would help me with my particular chemical imbalance. I tried Prozac, Zoloft, Nardil, Trazadone and many others. All worked for a few weeks or months but this control of my depression never lasted. My mania had been treated with anti-psychotics like Stelezine, Resperdal and Haldol to control the hallucinations. Anti-mania medications like Depakote and Lithium were also utilized. I continued to take daily medications but found no lasting relief for my mood swings.

It was around this time, I heard of a Jungian therapist in Lafayette, Louisiana, where I lived, and sought him out. Jungian principles and the Progoff workshop had instilled in me the hope that darkness, depression, and fantasies, even psychosis can be viewed as the psyche's attempt to heal itself. I had been unsuccessful so far in applying these concepts of self-treatment. This new therapist held hope for me even though it was with feelings of inadequacy that I approached him with a phone call. His name was Jason, and I have utilized him as a coach for my life and spirituality ever since. He was open to my sensitivity to God and allowed me to talk about this dimension of myself. Jason offered me skilled dream interpretation and psychotherapy on a weekly basis.

At first, I was cautious during therapy when I had to share my secret thoughts, fears, and fragile hopes. But Jason's non-judgmental approach put me at ease, as he encouraged me to be open. Dream interpretation using my conscious associations with dream images was foreign and a little awkward for me. But I found new energy for my depressive nature through this approach to bi-polar mental illness and was often eager for daily life after a therapy session. Understanding dreams and unlocking the energy in the symbols of the unconscious lead to a feeling of release and new-found dynamism.

Talking about the characters and symbols in a dream, and what they made me think of, meant discovering new thoughts about myself. I learned that the men in my dreams were expressions of the masculine side of my psyche. The feminine characters were expressions of my shadow side, the part of myself I denied. I found it encouraging when I learned that I had some strong positive female images within my personal makeup. Dreams about women such as certain nuns and nurses from my past that I admired led me to realize that the positive traits I saw in them were characteristics I had, but denied were a part of me. Courage and insight were the particular talents of these women in my dreams and past. Dream analysis taught me to acknowledge that these traits were really mine. Also, therapy and dreams helped me express all the deep sadness that filled my heart sometimes for reasons I could not explain. I began to feel heard and understood by someone for the first time in my life.

My psychiatrist while I was married to James disapproved of Jungian therapy. There were times when I mistakenly stopped my counseling with Jason at my psychiatrist's recommendation. In looking back, my only wish was that my psychiatrist and therapist would have been supportive of each other's attempts to bring wholeness into my life. Seeking the correct medication and therapy, along with solid connections to others, is the only way through bipolar mental illness. Their philosophies on therapy for mental illness were divergent. One believed only in medication and the other believed only in psychotherapy.

My psychiatrist would ask me, in our regular visits, how I felt. Her only purpose seemed to be to figure out what medication adjustment was needed. She did not seem to want an awareness of my inner search. She and my husband saw my mental workings as symptoms of illness, not expressions of a desperate searching soul who couldn't find her way without the help of a guide. The only hope they offered me was medication adjustments.

On the other hand, Jason was willing to spend an hour each week delving with me into the workings of my mind and heart. He listened to my journal writing. He was not afraid of, or impatient with my tears and hopeless feelings. He respected me by believing I was searching for a life of value. Psychoanalysis may take years, but it is through this genuine connection to another that one discovers authentic healing.

My psychiatrist recommended electroconvulsive therapy, shock treatments, for my unrelenting depression. The reason she recommended I stop Jungian therapy was that she believed it unearthed too much for me to deal with effectively. She never suggested that perhaps my husband or my father needed therapy. In 1988, I did stop seeing Jason and went through shock treatments at my husband's urging.

Electroconvulsive therapy (ECT) is a controversial treatment for severe depression that is still used at times today. While the client is under sedation, a small electric current is passed through the brain, causing a seizure. Through the use of padding, restraints and sedation, the client is protected from harm in this seizure. The effect of the treatment is to stop all higher thought patterns and allow the client to return to more practical thinking. It causes a person to temporarily lose short-term and some long-term memory. After the procedure, one is stunned and lost in a fog of forgetfulness. For me, weekly treatments were needed for several weeks.

I can't remember much of the details of my treatments. The short-term memory loss meant James had to reorient me to our home life after each treatment. Some of the long-term memory loss has lasted forever. I remember only bits and pieces of some events, like a trip to Europe I made in the late seventies, which is mostly gone from my memory.

ECT was like a death for me. My doctor attempted, in my mind, to use a knife to separate my conscious self from my past and this past's connection to the earth of my soul. It only served to introduce me to a jailed madwoman within me who had grown numb and dead to life. I identified with this jailed madwoman from my dreams and felt it was the clearest expression of me. Even though ECT enabled me to return from depression to all the activities of daily living, I walked like a zombie and felt myself to be cut off from all life within, and around me. I had stopped thinking of suicide, but was numb to life.

Months after shock treatments, I did begin to emerge as an individual with my own thoughts and emotions. I could make choices again. I was not depressed and objectively could see no hope for my marriage. Somehow James and I, though kind and gentle with each other, had failed one another as partners. Perhaps the age difference was the primary cause for the distance between us. I felt enough hope for myself to separate from him and start over again.

I chose to leave my psychiatrist and return to Jungian therapy. Somehow I knew this avenue would bring back to life what had been destroyed by the invasive logic of Western medicine with ECT. I believed at the time that there was no way around, under or over the dark depression within my soul. I believed that somewhere deep in the darkness of depression there was an authentic new life for me. I felt sure there was a way through this ugly mess within me, and my Jungian coach, Jason, believed the same thing.

In 1989, a year after ECT, I left my husband. I sought a future which was not clear in my mind. But I knew I did not belong with this positive father figure anymore. James believed in me, affirmed me, and even tried to protect me as a father should do. It was time for me to begin doing these things for myself. I felt I had to move away from him. I needed a masculine presence that I felt to be a peer. My search for home and belonging continued, and now it seemed focused on finding a man I perceived to be a savior, or hero and a peer. Still I had unrealistic views of real life situations and relationships. But I knew I needed a strong, grounded in reality, and creatively compassionate and insightful male figure in my life. I thought at this time, he would be someone from my outer world, a new husband. I had not yet discovered the positive masculine figure in my inner world and longed for his presence.

When I returned to treatment with Jason, our sessions were on a weekly basis. This therapist never seemed to view me as a mentally ill person. He treated me more as a troubled soul in search of new life. I live today without the label of mental illness and its stigma imprisoning me. He even taught me that frequently the people in the therapist's office are not the ones most in need of therapy. "Often," he said, "it's the people freely walking around without a conscience that are in need of the psychiatrist." By this statement, Jason referred to people who were so convinced of their authority and rightness that they had little regard for the thoughts and feelings of others, such as my father.

Because of the insights of Carl Jung and his followers, including my therapist, I view my inner madwoman as a friend, filled with power, potential and creativity. My conscious identity, my ego, is responsible for how I let this inner madwoman impact my life. Dream work enabled me to see images of the many facets of myself, the madwoman being one of them. I was able to acknowledge that my conscious identity was separate from this subconscious image of a mad witch. I learned to recognize when she was sad, angry or bitter. I began to deal lovingly with her, meeting her needs for expression through my art.

I eventually began to set boundaries on how she was allowed to impact my daily activities through depressive thoughts and manic behaviors. I gave her freedom of expression in my art. I would draw images of her from my dreams and imagination. I would imagine her as a person outside of me and say "No!" when I felt the urge to behave in a manic or depressed manner. Much of the anger, sadness or bitterness I knew became part of her rather than my conscious emotion. I began to see myself as normal with some mad forces in my subconscious with which I had to contend. I no longer saw myself as mad.

Through this active imagination, I would dialogue with the mad witch, hoping to understand her needs and purposes. Sometimes in this dialogue she would say how much she hated all men and revealed her jealousy for the power society gave them. I would acknowledge her feelings but then add how much I admired Jason. I would tell her that I wanted to give men a chance in my life and did not want to judge them without open experience of them in daily life. When she wanted to reject others I would counter her voice and energy with my attempts to be open. Other times when I drew images of her, she showed me her magical skills of playing with fire. I understood this to be the fire of imagination. She was a source of creative energy for me, and as the years went by, she served to spur me on in all my artistic endeavors. The important thing was that now I was conscious of her as a part of my unconscious make-up, and stopped her from controlling me from my subconscious.

I learned over the years that this approach to life that embraced the unconscious in regular Jungian therapy sessions worked to enable a spiritual healing that was nourishing and fruitful. This meant working with my dreams, fantasies, and active imagination. The thoughts, feelings and actions of my everyday life, past, present, and hoped-for future, were the meat of the therapy sessions. Dream analysis had to be done weekly. This style of therapy takes years, and it is not until the next phase of my journey that you will see its full impact on my personal and professional life with good problem-solving skills.

I propose that active imagining, dream analysis, journaling and artistic endeavors are the components of a Jungian spirituality. They have led to a deeper connection with God as I find this evolving reality expressed in my particular soul and journey. This approach to life is rich with texture and vitality. At times, active imagining, dream work and art have haunted me with the desire to understand more, but they have always inspired me to seek the fulfillment of my life dreams for mental health and wholeness.

The major tasks for me in therapy were to talk about the masculine and feminine influences in my life journey. This included experiences of rape, both psychological and physical. I had to learn to deal responsibly with my own inner critic and particularly to stop devaluing my emotions. My dreams also gave me direct exposure to the negative masculine energy within me, seen in the images of men abusing women. I had to confront these inner critics that came from all the negative masculine influences in my personal journey and in the dominating patriarchal society of the Western world.

In the early stages of dream work, I would deal with images of several men, often cowboys, treating a woman or myself in a rough, possessive manner. Frequently, I dreamed of riding in a car with a man or my father driving. I learned from Jason that these were images of how the masculine side of my psyche was treating my nature, roughly and possessively. I learned that the critical and demanding personality of my father was in the driver's seat of my life.

Soon I began to recognize the male voices in my thought patterns that were aimed at devaluing and criticizing my attempts to live. When I would think thoughts like, "You can't do that!" or "That would be a stupid thing to do!" I would immediately imagine the negative male figure from my dreams, and tell him "No, you are not allowed to speak to me that way." Eventually my inner negative critics were less intense with less impact on my shy nature. I began to think more positively about my actions and myself. I would affirm myself as valuable because of the strong compassion that was part of my nature. This positive affirming approach to my behaviors resulted in more positive nighttime dreams. Soon, in my car dreams, I was in the driver's seat.

My therapist, who worked with me, even up to the present day, became a new positive masculine energy that valued, honed, and uplifted me. Jason's office was decorated with a library of books on one wall and art on the other walls. African masks, colorful spiral forms and mandala-images were some of the art he chose. Pictures of his family also presented an image of a creative, loving masculine approach to life. He taught me to take seriously and prioritize my feelings in every situation. He helped me identify the values I cherished most. Subsequently, this led me to make choices for greater balance and self-worth. Over the years, I chose to keep friends and family close to me. In repeated sessions, he also taught me to identify, understand and set boundaries on the differences between real perceptions and illusions or delusions, such as paranoia. Once when I was working as a nurse, I felt stressed by feelings of judgment and rejection by other staff. Jason helped me sort out real expressions from others from my own perceptions based on fantasy and imagination. In this situation, no one had verbally expressed this rejection, but I had intuited it based on facial expressions. I learned these facial movements could or could not have been directly meant to communicate a message of judgment towards me. I choose to see these facial expressions as revealing more about the person himself or herself than about how they felt about me.

In Jungian therapy, it is the unconscious that does the healing, but the conscious self does the work. Jason's philosophy of therapy embraced the subconscious with precision and skill and he taught me to do the same. As my story continues in the final phase of my journey, you will see more clearly how depression, art, and Jungian therapy worked together to bring out a wholesome and balanced life for me.

Third Phase of my life: Part II:
Depression and Its Beauty

Chapter IX: Dafney Street, Art School, and Family

When I divorced James in 1989, I was a marginalized member of society on Social Security Disability for my mental illness. I lived in a home on Dafney Street in Lafayette, a home James lovingly bought for me. This house was white with a green roof, green shutters on the windows, three bedrooms and a lovely back porch. The neighborhood was middle class with passing acquaintances for neighbors. We all waved to each other as we greeted the beginning of our day or as we came home in the evening. But there were no other social interactions between us. I cherished this home as it gave me a solid financial foundation on a low income. This home was to be my sole grounding for ten years until I moved to live with Ron, my present husband. These years were an important period for inner stability, with growing commitment and ability to be responsible for myself. It seems I should have learned this long before my forties. Commitment to a lifestyle that included self-control and a permanent relationship with another was always out of my reach.

I held the dream of being a wife and mother close to my heart. Motherhood now seemed no longer possible. Being divorced and unable to hold a job at forty due to bi-polar disease left me feeling like a failure. I felt great shame for my inability to express nourishment and care for myself or another I chose to love. Tears from the overwhelming feelings of sadness over all these failures in life marked my first night in this new home.

All through my years on Dafney, I continued Jungian therapy. The road to mental health would be long and difficult, covering a ten-year period. Jason was very helpful, and affirming of my search for well-being. But the work of applying Jungian principles to my life was up to me. This work was complex and demanding. I did not experience healing at first.

Alternating bouts of depression and mania had to be faced and eventually managed, and this was the task of my life while on Dafney. I chose to turn one room into an art studio where I drew and painted, yelled and cried, destroyed and created over and over again, images from dreams, active imagination and fantasies. There were images that related to the dismemberment of men and this allowed me to express the long- suppressed, justified rage I felt towards all the harsh, violating masculine figures from my earlier life. Reliving the rape I experienced in my college years, through guided imagery and active imagination during a therapy session, allowed me to see the injustice done to me. My innocence and justified rage surfaced in my art. I drew pictures of attacks on negative men from my dreams. I destroyed paintings I made of dark masculine figures. There was one painting of a young woman with her head twisted upwards and her eyes squinting as she gazed painfully at the viewer. She was surrounded by dark images of men's bodies that appeared to be haunting her with their darkness. I smashed or pulled the head off of sculptures of masculine dream figures that kept criticizing me. Destruction of masculine images allowed a safe place for the expression of this rage.

I had a new psychiatrist whom Jason recommended. His name was Randal. He greeted me with a bold handshake and direct eye contact as he said, "I hear you are looking for help with your mood swings." He was warm and positive in his manner while his build was big and bulky. He acknowledged to me that he knew some of my relatives on my father's side of the family, and he was intimately involved in their struggles with bi-polar mental illness. He said no more but did give me the impression that he understood my father's aggressive nature as part of my family history. This was the first time a medical professional led me to understand that my illness was not solely in me but that others in my family needed as much therapy as I did to get well. He believed I could make it out of depression. Randal worked with my mood swings, changing my medications, struggling with me to find a balance with which I could live. He also respected Jason. Their connection enabled me to relate to each of them with hope and expectancy.

I tried to go to art school, hoping to attain an art therapy degree. I did well in art classes until I encountered, over a winter semester break, a deep darkness after a period of successful sculpturing. I had done well in the fall sculpturing class, making several images of women. I ranked high in the class grading system. Yet, I became arrogant towards a male student with whom I was competitive. As the semester ended, I even confronted the teacher as showing favoritism towards this male student. My arrogance was rude in its expression to my fellow student and the teacher. I challenged both of them openly at an end-of-semester party. I made a fool of myself and hurt them with my verbal attacks.

My creative energies in this sculpturing class were early expressions of mania. In the early stages of a manic episode, one finds that the ideas and energy to carry out these ideas come easily. But this experience with success can escalate and spin out of control, resulting in chaos. I could not keep up with the racing thoughts and mental stimuli that came my way as I worked to create these feminine images. One sculpture was of a large abstract image of a woman's body, another of a flashy female prostitute. A third one was an abstract image of a maze of shapes that was called, "The Wedding Night." I dialoged with each of these sculptures, trying to understand where they came from within me and what they meant to me. What did I think of my body, prostitution, and marriage? Was a woman meant for more than this or are these images somehow expressions of a woman's greatness? This kind of thinking to myself as I created these and other images flashed through my brain at a speed that only confused me. This led to frustration that I took out on this student and teacher. I never saw these two individuals again and did not resolve this incident with an apology or explanation.

During the winter break that followed this fall class, I experienced a depression, feeling guilty for my judgmental behaviors towards my sculpting class.   I feared the creative skills within me, feared they would only step on others on my road to the top. I would rather be an unknown, ineffective person who hurts no one than a successful person who abuses others. I was in a mental hospital for the full two weeks of the semester break. I had admitted myself because thoughts of wanting to kill myself were constantly pressuring me and causing intense anxiety. In these two weeks, my medication was changed and I talked about my shame and fears of my own thinking processes. I gained balance and some hope I could return to school. But I was still shaken with anxiety about my creative energies.

I returned to school in January to a woodcarving class and froze with fear before the knife and the wood. Trembling, I put the knife down. I still had negative inner critics with whom I had to do battle. I was not ready to handle the inner knife of differentiation on my own, because my positive inner hero had not yet proved himself as capable of this skill. **Differentiation** is the ability to separate facts and values in a given situation so that one can make choices. Cutting on the beautiful piece of wood frightened me. It meant knowing what was to be thrown away and what had to be saved in order to make a solid image. I knew I was not yet capable of this in my personal life. I feared I could only cut and destroy.

At this point, the little girl dressed in red who had emerged in my first psychotic event while on the retreat came to my mind. She was the one who could control the bullish, critical masculine thinking in my psyche. In one of my dreams, it was this child who confronted the charging bull, grounding him to the lying position by a simple pull of his penis to the earth. This dream symbol held healing energy for me, and though I still cannot do much with it logically, it often brings me great peace in life. As a painting I did in my art studio, this image of the child and the bull was often on my mind. I kept this painting on a wall in my bathroom so that several times a day I would gaze at it in privacy and experience the mystery of these opposing images. The powerless child and the charging bull held great energy. Somehow, my subconscious brought them together in a single image that was peaceful and healing. In the image, the child became powerful and the bull became calm. I had the hope that somehow in time, I would gain the ego strength to curtail my negative, critical logic and witness the corralling of the bull. As yet this had not happened.

While in the woodcarving class, I realized the bullishness of my critical negative thinking could not be trusted to wield the knife of discrimination between the delicate realities I found in my soul through my artwork. In art and counseling, my sensitive nature towards God and others had surfaced. But often I would condemn myself as self-centered and unworthy of anything good. I could not choose which of these feelings was fact or fiction, which was valuable and which had to be discarded. Was I worthy of anything good? Was I really a sensitive woman with a real connection to God? In art class, my inner critic would devalue my feelings and condemn me as self-centered. This inner criticism of my artistic efforts led me to destroy and abandon projects. Hence, in the second semester, this inner tension led me to quit art school.

I remember another episode, during this time in my life. I was visiting my sister and had been talking with Jason on the phone about troubling dreams and feelings. When I got off the phone, I spoke, in a manic-like soliloquy with disjointed sentences, of my inner struggle with logic, images and feelings. I spoke both out loud to myself and to the family gathered at my sister's home. I was suddenly grabbed by my four extremities and carried to a police car to be committed to a mental hospital. It all happened so fast I was in the police car before I realized there had been a person grabbing each of my arms and legs. I was in shock. When I got to the mental hospital, I consented to a voluntary admission, as I knew I was out of control. I did not have to be committed against my will.

I was in the hospital for two weeks, as I was for most hospitalizations for depression. The secure environment of a mental hospital was comforting to me and the staff affirmed my ability to speak in ways that made sense to the listener. My medication was adjusted and this manic episode was resolved without much difficulty.

There is, in looking back, recognition of a loving presence in this gesture from my brothers and sisters to commit me to a hospital. They simply felt at a loss of how to help me. They feared where I was heading with my racing, incoherent thoughts and lack of self-care. At the time, I felt only the loss of my identity and freedom as a person.

My inner search and struggles that made sense to me were only signs of illness to others. My feelings at the time of admission were frustration and helplessness. But in the hospital, I met others who had similar problems as I did and I slowly learned to accept my disability.

There are no simple rules for a family to follow in attempting to reach out to a member who is struggling with mental illness. I wish for me there had been in my family a gentle listening presence but I realize this is hard to do when confronted with insanity and incoherence. Never having had children leaves me without much to recommend to the family of an adult mentally ill person. I believe strongly that a gentle approach is essential, but the responsibility of coping with the illness lies ultimately with the ill person alone. I would recommend to any family the National Alliance on Mental Illness, NAMI. Though I never worked with them, NAMI offers support and classes for families of the mentally ill.

I have had friends in the last few years who approached me about how to deal with their mentally ill adult children. I wish my parents or brothers and sisters would have sought Jungian therapy for themselves in order to understand the archetypes and myths that energize their behaviors and relationships. This awareness might have helped them set boundaries on their own inner world. My father might have gained insight to his aggressive, judgmental views towards me. This insight could have led him to see his views and aggressive behaviors as projections of his own soul's complexity. We might have experienced more compassion and understanding between us in our communications.

Distance with my family had one good impact on my life. I was forced to independence and personal responsibility for my mental illness. I chose to interact little with my family during my struggle with bipolar depression. This isolation, particularly while I lived on Dafney, forced me to take responsibility for my life, which meant accepting my role as the key controller of my destiny. This enabled me to deal with my failures in relating to others and myself in a constructive manner. There was no one to blame for my failures. I had to learn to work positively with my weaknesses.

My struggle with depression was particularly strong in the first years of my life on Dafney Street and suicidal thoughts were almost always with me. I felt that hanging myself or taking an overdose would relieve my suffering. But I was to learn that this was not a healthy way to face my problems.

Chapter X: Suicide Attempt and the Choice for Life

After the hospitalization during art school, there were two or three more hospitalizations, usually during the fall and winter for suicidal thinking. The circumstances leading to admission for the hospitalization during 1991 is gone from my memory. Hospitalization was a repeated event where memories of them often melted into one. But they were mostly during the winter over my birthday and the Christmas holidays. Most years, I celebrated my birthday and Christmas with no one and loneliness was always a profound factor. In 1992, I actually did attempt suicide, but with the help of my sister, I lived on to discover new life from this depth of despair.

One evening I went out for dinner with friends. This was a family I worked for cleaning house. I was in need of more income and sought work as a housekeeper. With weekly visits to clean, I became familiar with both Cathy and her husband, Tony. We went to a Cajun food restaurant and spent the evening talking about how they met as a couple. They talked about how their family and work life had developed. They met at a bar several years ago playing pool as competitors. They had jobs in construction and bookkeeping that paid their bills and allowed them to enjoy trips to neighboring places like New Orleans for overnight fun in the city. They had two children and even though the wife had severe arthritis from an early age, they were happy as a family. I was moved by the intimacy and genuine friendship of this couple with whom I spent the evening.

Coming home to my empty house, I felt such a sharp contrast between the happiness of the couple and my lonely life on Dafney Street. I felt sad and angry at my circumstances. I began to talk with the inner figure Hermes, who I had read about in Jungian books and whom Jason had mentioned briefly in a therapy session. Hermes was presented as a trickster and magician that assisted individuals with transition times in life. He also is particularly present when one crosses the fine line between the conscious and unconscious worlds, like when falling asleep at night. Hermes was a figure in Greek mythology who was a messenger, magician and musician. Murray Stein in his book, *In Midlife, A Jungian Perspective,* presents this archetype as the guiding force for people in transition such as in midlife of adulthood. His presence is always mysterious and vague, hard to recognize in dreams and fantasies. But the energy of this archetype tries to guide and befriend one through dark and difficult periods.

In my mind, this tiny, impish figure sat on my shoulder and told me the only way through my depression was in taking a bottle of pills.

He assured me the pills would not hurt me. I followed his instructions without thinking through this imaginary dialogue. I failed to bring this fantasy to a session with Jason. I should have written the dialog in my journal and then waited until I saw Jason again to discuss what this inner figure was trying to say to me. Because I did not do this, I missed the opportunity to discover an in-depth understanding of the dying of the ego desires that is necessary for any real growth. Perhaps what Hermes was trying to get me to do was to let go of my old fantasies of husband and children and focus more on my potential as a single woman. I misunderstood the inner dialog with this imaginary figure and began to take the pills. After swallowing over two hundred pills of Nardil and Resperdal, I began to fall asleep.

In and out of consciousness, I knew death awaited me. In a moment of clarity, I called from this dark experience to my sister. I don't know what I told her, but Marie sent the police and ambulance to my home. These men of service courageously broke the front window to get into the house. I was not conscious of their coming in or putting me on the stretcher. They took me to University Medical Center. I did regain consciousness briefly while in the emergency room. Two of my sisters were beside me. Their loving smiles connected me to the healing feminine forces around me. After a few days being stabilized there, I spent two weeks in a mental hospital getting my medication adjusted. Then I spent a month living with my family. When I felt brave and strong enough mentally to return home, I was discharged to my own care.

When I finally returned home, my knees shook as I walked into my house. The broken window illuminated the dark dimension of my psyche and confronted my wish to live alone and be independent. I seemed incapable of handling my inner and outer life in any organized and acceptable manner. Yet, I was alone and Dafney Street was my home.

My lifestyle at this time was marked by a growing awareness of a repeated weakness in my personality. Periods of mania, often occurring in the spring, with excessive thinking, rationalism and racing ideas, caused me to overstep the boundaries of my capacity in finances and friendship. One spring, I spent seventeen thousand dollars on costume jewelry and cosmetics. This was money I had saved from my marriage to James. It was all gone in a heartbeat. During these periods of mania, I was outspoken and rude to friends and men I dated such as I was in art school. I met men through a newspaper-advertising agency. I would make a recording of what I was like and what I was looking for in a male partner. Interested men would leave me a message with their contact information and I would chose to call them back or not. One man I met was about my age and a successful oil businessman. We got along visiting at a local pub. But when he encountered my opinionated and often disjointed thinking about the world economy and politics, he backed away from me. He would not answer his phone when I called. Quickly I lost what few connections I was making with others. This was followed by a fall in mood and a lack of relating to life around me during the winter months.

I grappled in therapy with the wounds to my feminine nature by an overbearing father, the hoped-filled engagement that ended in rejection, and the rape from my college years. The subconscious imagery from these experiences was negative and overpowering. Dreams about my father or Richard were always sad for me. I often dreamed of being overtaken by a cloud or veil that imprisoned me, reminding me of the drugged fog I was in when raped.

For about three or four years, during the Christmas holidays and over my winter-birthday, I was in a mental hospital for depression. I accepted visits from no one while in the hospital, still unable to allow myself to connect with another when overcome with depression and the sadness of winter. There is a type of depression known as Seasonal Affective Disorder and I tried to treat myself with the light therapy this illness required. The rationale behind this illness is that lack of adequate sunlight in the winter causes one to have an imbalance of the chemical melatonin. Melatonin helps with the cycle of wake and sleep. Lack of adequate sleep also leads to daytime depression. I ordered a large florescent lamp source that I sat in front of for several hours a day. I did not find significant help from this effort and abandoned it after several months.

After a few years of this pattern of mood swings in winter and spring, with the help of medication, therapy and art, I was able to step out of myself and see this winter gloom for what it was, a cyclical dying within me and the world of nature. I had to learn to recognize and control my reactions to this seasonal happening. With the dying of the leaves and all the green of summer, and the lessening of daylight, I too sank into a dying type of existence. But even though the leaves die, I began to recognize that the tree lives on and spring returns.

This winter darkness in my soul was like the Greek story of **Persephone**, who was stolen by the underworld and had to return cyclically to the depths of Hades and the subconscious. When I took ownership for this Greek story being played out in my life, it was a big step towards integration of my personality with the world at large. I had to learn to confront this repeated darkness and prevent it from destroying my daily life.

This was an important awareness. It was Jason, my therapist, who pointed out to me the similarity between Persephone and my repeated bouts with mania in the spring and depression in the winter. I learned to observe my moods objectively by seeing them reflected in the Greek story. Slowly, I learned to embrace dark mood swings as an opportunity to relate to myself with love and acceptance. I began trusting I would discover the light of Spring through these meditative embraces of my dark feelings.

A sharp turn of events led me to gain a self-willed control of my inner and outer perceptions. It was a choice for life.

In the early months of 1993, I had developed the delusion that the police were after me because I had been found guilty of killing my brothers, sisters and parents. I felt I should kill myself. This obsessive fear had me wiping my fingerprints from everything I touched. Fear and anxiety drove me to a self-admission to a psychiatric hospital for these delusions and suicidal thoughts.

While there, a fear of losing my home to fire filled me with tension. I wanted desperately to leave the hospital against medical advice to go home and turn off the fans I had left on. I feared they would cause a fire. My doctor addressed the fear by telling me to call someone to check on the fans. I felt I had no one that I could call. I knew I had to go myself even though the hospital told me I could not leave.

This personal responsibility for a simple everyday reality, turning off electrical appliances when not in use, challenged me to contain the dark unconscious energies that repeatedly wrecked my life and footing in society. I decided to accept responsibility for my daily practical treasures, particularly my home and lifestyle on Dafney. I did leave against medical advice and ever since have chosen to separate my conscious identity from, yet be responsible for, the dark powerful unconscious energy I carry in my soul and psyche. Though my thinking about the dangers of fans running unsupervised in my home may have been deluded, this choice for care of my home life over care for my psychic life was an important change of focus in my thinking. No longer was I to let my distorted thinking have the power to make me forget about the practical responsibilities of everyday life.

Leaving the hospital without the support of the staff made me accept my crucial responsibility of never attempting suicide or harming another person because I had allowed fears and distorted thinking or images free run in my conscious mind. Standing alone, I became committed to facing my mental illness in a new way, a path that would allow me to confine those subconscious energies and channel them away from the destruction of my home life and place in society. I was not sure how to do this, but I was convinced that I had to be stronger than these forces and learn to direct them into creative and life-giving endeavors.

Where this determination to stop the destructiveness of my mental illness came from, I do not know for sure. I just know that fear of losing my home to fire caused me to say "no" to a lifestyle of repeated bouts with depression and mania. I was fed up with its negative power and decided there had to be a way other than hospitalization or suicide. I was determined to find a new way of living. Perhaps some divine spark within me brought me to this turning point.

From this point on, I focused on being in charge of and responsible for all the fiery or depressed images and moods that came over me. I was tired of being robbed of my life by the subconscious. So in 1993, I began the painful task of overcoming fears that kept me from success as a nurse and a woman in society. I began looking for work and even repeated failures in jobs did not stop me from seeking an expression of my compassionate connection to others who suffered physically and emotionally. One job I tried was working as a psychiatric nurse. In the second week on the job, a mental patient that was out of control confronted me. Not realizing I was standing in the doorway, the only means of escape for this desperate patient, I became an added threat to her. She lunged towards me, attacked me and broke two of my ribs. With feelings of incompetence, I quit that job immediately. Another position was working as a teacher in a school for LPN's. LPN's or sometimes known as LVN's, are licensed practical nurses that assist

RN's with nursing duties. After working in this setting for two months, I began to feel the other teachers and principal were scrutinizing my teaching skills. I felt I was about to be fired. I quit before I found out if this was paranoia or justified fear. Quitting revealed my anxiety about my performance and my fears of rejection and failure.

After losing three jobs due to inadequate on-the-job performance, I secured weekend work in a rehab facility. I spent six years working as a nurse in this long-term care rehabilitation center where I channeled my compassionate energy and grew slowly, gaining confidence as a nurse. Working only two days a week allowed me five days to cope with the pressures of work. This way of living led to my stability on the job.

Paranoia and emotional stress were the particular personal challenges I had to deal with in this search for a professional life. These psychological inadequacies had to be channeled into painting and sculpturing endeavors. I frequently feared that others were watching me and criticizing my nursing performances. I could not tell whether this was paranoia or fact and it led to much anxiety. Therapy with Jason helped me with this differentiation.

Often after work, I would paint images of people and situations I feared and would talk with these images. I drew abstract images of the emotions these dialogues developed. Sometimes, the emotions were anger and frustration that I drew in reds and blacks with jagged lines and sharp angles. Other times, the colors were meant to express mixtures of joy and fear at the same time. These were many-colored paintings that showed divergent lines, both curved and jagged. Putting the paranoia and anxiety on paper helped me to objectify them and then talk about them in therapy. Jason helped me talk about the separate emotions and what facts from my workday may have contributed to these emotions. Old emotional wounds from my past were separated from the current feelings of inadequacy with nursing skills. Jason taught me to give the wounds time to heal and to give myself time to practice new nursing skills. I learned to separate my inner fears from my self-expressions at work. It took the entire five days I was off to deal with the two days of interactions with patients and staff. During the two days I worked, I was nervous and fearful, but when I was off I would console myself with this inner work, affirm my attempts to be a working member of society, and commit to my tasks as a nurse.

Fears related to injections of medications, caused me to tremble physically. I felt nervous drawing up the correct dose in the syringe and tremors made me anxious about giving the injection. I feared hurting the client. I had to learn to handle the intrusive, painful events of my own history and personality while trying to perform these simple, daily tasks. It was not easy professionally or personally.

In the past, I had situations where I developed anxiety created by the assertive questioning by insightful psychiatrists. My first psychiatrist in 1978 asked me a point blank question that caused me to hide in fear, as I was not ready to deal with it. He simply asked, "Do you have lots of issues with your father?" His question felt like a knife in my stomach and I immediately closed down in his therapy session. His approach to therapy seemed bullish to me. Working as a nurse, I feared the bullish power of my own critical thinking to churn the guts of others with my intuitive insights to their natures. I knew I had a tendency to assume I knew what was wrong with other people and try to correct it. I did not want to be bullish towards others because I was scarred by the same attitude of others towards me. I had to learn to separate these inner fears of causing pain to another from the invasive nursing tasks such as injections that were meant to enhance healing in another.

I did not feel I was a good nurse, but I did begin to take pride in simple gestures of compassion. This focus allowed me to calm myself when I had to give injections to my patients. Though today I am not comfortable with all nursing skills, I did learn, at this time in my life, to express my desire for professional success. I have gained the ability to learn new skills without overwhelming fear hindering me.

The development of these objective and persevering skills along with my spiritual nature was an important development in my psyche and led to my overall success as a nurse. These were good inner masculine traits that meant my inner-man was beginning to relate better to me. This positive inner-man began to show up in my dreams, reaching out to me and affirming me. I would dream about men from my everyday life that I admired for their sensitivity, compassion and critical thinking skills. One was of a doctor I worked with and in the dream he approached me with a gesture of intimacy. In these dreams, these men reflected my strong masculine side that wanted to lead me to deeper and more successful connection to myself in both my inner and outer worlds.

In therapy, I learned to quickly distinguish the positive masculine principle in my psyche from the negative dimensions of this facet of the unconscious. Jane Wheelwright, in her book *For Women Growing Older, The Animus*, describes the impact of the negative masculine energy and the positive masculine. Negatively, the male figure in one's psyche makes a woman opinionated, domineering and argumentative, while positively, he makes her objective, persevering and spiritual. This masculine principle in a woman's psyche is called the **animus.** I was beginning to develop a positive animus over and against the negative one that had dominated my life for so many years. The **anima** is the female principle in a man's psyche and is most often seen in his dreams and imagination. You would have to refer to Jungian writers for an explanation of how this aspect of a man's unconscious impacts his personality positively and negatively. The one book I am aware of is called "*He*" by Robert Johnson. I am sure there are many others, in fact much of Jung's writings elaborate in detail the impact of the anima on a man's consciousness.

After quitting art school, I spent an extensive amount of time in my studio at home. Here I discovered in my nighttime dreams and daytime artistic creations, a strong loving feminine deity that sought me out, strengthened, embraced and challenged me to love myself by wrestling with my shadow side. My shadow side was revealed in images of the wounded feminine, and the witch and madwoman. These images were revealed daily in my art, dreams and fantasies.

In one dream, this feminine deity was perceived as the moon chasing me, when suddenly the image changed and I was wrestling with a dark figure that cried out "What's in it for me?" I understood this dream to be a call from the divine to reason with my shadow side, to show empathy towards it and to gain the upper hand in managing it. I did this by drawing images of the wounded feminine aspects of my life, particularly the bitter witch and the lonely madwoman. I chose to relate to them with patience, compassion, and objectivity. I frequently drew a picture of the madwoman with someone combing her hair as a way of showing her compassion and help in straightening out her thoughts. I would not let these feminine images express their negative feelings in my life except in my artistic creations. Painting the mad witch with her hair gone wild and playing with fire allowed this mad side to be validated but not acted upon. I learned in therapy to begin to separate their sadness or bitterness from my own conscious identity and behaviors.

This image of the moon as the divine feminine has always moved me emotionally. I view her as loving and subtly powerful. I call her "Mama." While in art school, I made a sculpture of this divine feminine. It was a life-size, abstract figure of an adult woman with large hips and breasts. I was able to fully embrace it, which I did every morning and evening in a prayerful gesture for many years while I lived on Dafney Street. In this gesture, I found consolation and hope, especially for panic attacks that had surfaced during this time in my life.

Panic attacks seem to come from nowhere. Suddenly overtaken by an anxiety of impending doom, I would experience a racing heart and breath pattern. Trembling, I felt as though I was sliding down a slippery slope to my immediate death. These attacks of anxiety would happen in a calm day with no causative event. Sometimes, they would occur just as I was preparing to go out for the day, revealing my fears of life outside my home. Only by embracing this sculpture of the divine feminine was I able to calm the attack. This gesture would allow the anxiety to pass.

The Hermes-like energy within that I had misunderstood as an invitation to suicide now was to be encountered as this figure's healing, creative, insightful capacities from within my own subconscious. I remember in 1996 sitting alone in the living room of my home and just being in the quiet and darkness, waiting hopefully for new life.

I would sit in peace with a nighttime dream of mine. In this dream, a young boy dressed in blue would play his flute. With the multicolored music that flowed from his horn, he would drive away a massive, white, intruding Mack truck that charged toward me down a long dark corridor from my childhood home. I made a painting of this dream and it held much healing power. The dream brought to mind my first memory of my father's harsh discipline, the driveway experience when we moved into our new home on Lake Arthur Avenue. In this memory, my father sharply, harshly disciplined me to quiet down my excitement over the new house. In reflecting on this dream, I found healing for all the childhood memories where too much masculine criticism and strength wounded the delicate female child in me.

I would sit with this painting and sing to myself the nursery rhyme, "little boy blue come blow your horn, the sheep are in the meadow and the cows are in the corn." With this quiet singing, I gained a calm, hopeful, waiting attitude towards the healing of my mental illness and my sensitive nature towards the dark subconscious energy that often overwhelmed me, as it had done in the story of Persephone.

Through the symbolic presence of Hermes, as the small boy dressed in blue, I learned to corral my instinctive, intuitive imagination that often forced me to act without restraint. This imagination was like the cows and sheep let out of the barn and destroying the meadow. The song and music of the little boy dressed in blue brought me peace, as I used active imagination to bring the cows and sheep home to the barn.

The great power, the masculine energy, found in criticism and my father's aggressiveness, represented by the white Mack truck, was pushed back with music from the flute of Hermes. This dream revealed the power of music as it prevented the forceful negative masculine from overrunning my life. No logic or reasoning was involved in this healing. Only a peaceful, consistent mindfulness of the imagery of the dream was necessary.

This experience with music as a healing force reminded me of Pachelbel's *Canon* that calmed me when I had my first psychotic event. So at this time in my life, I would listen to the *Canon* as it gave me hope and helped heal my soul in a way no medication or rational thinking could have ever done.

My home became a secluded place for me where I grew in personal integrity while I slowly developed a role in society as a nurse and a single woman. It took the years from 1989 to 1999 for me to gain a calm feminine expression in everything I chose to do. Manic and depressive periods became less intense and less disruptive. People found me easier to be around as I learned to open up and share myself without being overly withdrawn or dramatic. Deep genuine friendship slowly became possible, as friends like Jill and my sisters developed relationships with me. Struggles and disagreements were no longer the end of a relationship. They became only bumps in the road that added texture to the friendship. Stable relationships mark the next part of my journey.

Chapter XI: Stable Relationships

Jill was a woman who rented a room from me while I lived on Dafney. At first, I needed her only for financial reasons because my Social Security Disability Income was not sufficient to cover my monthly expenses. Jill also struggled to find work. Over the few years we lived together, we became close. We began to share morning prayer time. Rising early before dawn, we would sit on the back porch and read the psalms from the Bible together. This gave both of us great hope and peace towards the difficulties in our lives.

Jill was a hard-working woman, who had a lighthearted approach to life. She often laughed and saw the ironies in life. She helped me to take life a little less seriously. She too was in her forties, divorced and without children or family. Yet, she was mostly happy in her outlook on life.

She worked as a maid in the homes of rich people. All the while, she wanted work in the field of her training, which was bookkeeping.

She came home each day, exhausted from cleaning other people's houses. Daily, she would apply for better jobs, and eventually found a good position with a local ambulance company as a bookkeeper. She was very proud of her accomplishment because, with this job, she added security to her life.

Jill accepted me and my mood swings. She encouraged me in my slow progress with mental illness. Often, she would say, "I think you are getting better." In 1999, when I moved to live with Ron, my husband, Jill moved into her own apartment. We have remained close friends even to this day. I don't know what enabled Jill to accept and validate me. I suppose her own struggles in finding a place in society made her especially compassionate towards me. She was sensitive to my mood swings, and on a daily basis helped me to identify early stages of sadness or hypomania. She was the first person to see my advances in managing my mental illness. I am grateful that she came into my life. She was also the one who encouraged me to be patient with, and less judgmental towards the men I dated. She helped me accept the movement of Ron into my life.

Dating and the development of a relationship with Ron was a major achievement in this part of my journey. I met Ron in a coffee shop one early January morning in 1994. He sat at a table near me and I approached him with a simple question about how his day was going. We began a conversation about our lives and he moved over to my table. We shared for several hours and then made plans to go out that evening for supper. He had, six months earlier, lost his wife to a sudden illness, and I was open to his story of grief and pain. He was sort of quiet yet open and talkative. My compassion started him talking but our attraction kept us talking beyond his grief. We talked for hours that first day. He had moved from Berkeley, California with his wife, Ginger. He worked as a dental technician who made crowns and bridges for dentists, while she was an at-home kindergarten teacher. He was devastated when she was taken by ambulance to the nearby hospital. While she was taken by ambulance, he saw to it that the kindergarten children got home. When he was able to get to the emergency room, she had already died. The following days and the funeral filled his life with tears and shock. Family and friends from California came and spent time with Ron, encouraging him to see the future with hope. Within months of her death, he was able to begin a search for new life. It had been a happy marriage and Ron was hoping he would one day re-establish a relationship with a caring woman.

Ron had a degree in fine art and we shared a love for art. We grew first as friends. He introduced me to oil paintings in museums and challenged me to try it. Soon, I began to realize that in my life story during my years on Dafney, he was the only stable male relationship. From 1994 onward, when I looked around he was always there.

The course of the relationship between Ron and me was not easy or smooth, but it was consistent. I decided in 1994, I was going to make this friendship with Ron last. This was the same time in my life when I chose to live with better control of my mental illness and to seek work as a nurse. Though I chose to be committed to him long before he made a conscious commitment to me, he was the consistent one in our relationship. He had a few behaviors I rejected, like being a smoker. He was also very practical and connected to reality. He did not wander in thoughts about God, society, or politics as I did, but was outspoken about how a place or person looked. His observations with his senses were keen, the exact opposite of my intuitive nature. He was always there and never left me, regardless of my rejecting opinions about him. This was the saving factor for our relationship and for my life of belonging. Though we separated several times because of my judgmental rejection of him, he remained available to me. Luckily, I cherished his persistent openness.

His strong practical awareness of reality challenged my intuitive approach to life. This was often the source of our disagreements. He could see my lack of connection to reality in simple things like forgetting to close cupboard doors. I was more concerned with how much feeling I put into a painting or expressed in a day's interactions. He put more emphasis on how orderly our home was kept. He would confront my numb presence to reality and this angered me. Together we would work out these opposing perceptions. At first, we sought distance with disagreements. Slowly, we began talking about our different values and ways of seeing life. We each began to change, becoming more tolerant of each other's weaknesses. Jill, in particular, supported me in this new relationship, and encouraged me to accept him and not be so critical of him.

Though there have been times in the eighteen years of our relationship when Ron and I almost separated, I always chose to stay with him. The bull in me wisely has chosen to say no to my thoughts of leaving Ron behind as I journey forward. At first, my choice to stay with him led me into a sadness that endured for a year. We had married by this time and I had become disillusioned with his potential as my partner. His smoking and opinions about how our home should look and be organized burdened me. I became depressed when we moved to California in 2003. My separation from family and the familiarity of Louisiana and Dafney Street added to my sadness.

During this first year in California, the bullish, critical energy in me, that wanted to leave Ron, emerged transformed as a hero that secured for me a healing bond between Ron and myself. Daily saying yes to him and his gentle presence eventually led me to trust and genuinely love him.   In time, I discovered in our relationship a welding together of the masculine and feminine energies within my soul.

I spent many early morning hours with the painting of the tiny girl in the red dress and the charging bull. This child in her powerless stature held the bull still until he was calm and no longer charging to run or destroy. My active imagination with these figures grounded and tamed the masculine energy in me that was critical of Ron. I did not accomplish this through tough mindedness. It was a gift from the struggle with depression. The healing energy in the image of the child who has the power to gentle and ground the bull had a calming impact on me and my need to run. This image of the child is truly a **divine child**. She had powers that a real child of such a young age would not possess.

I do not know where this sometimes-rocky relationship with Ron is headed, but I know it will always be grounding for me. It enabled me to accept the many dark facets of my personality, and gave me the stability to grow in my capacity to creatively handle these energies. It is as though he created the container for all my dimensions, dark and beautiful, that never had a home. What he saw in me, I cannot imagine. What I gave to him, other than a place for him just to be, is again out of my awareness. He is the quiet, patient, simple masculine that I needed to balance the critical, exacting, and forceful masculine I had within me.

Ron witnessed my mood swings, but expressed his belief that bi-polar was nothing more than a measure of one's sensitive nature. He felt I was no different than others, except that my emotions were more exaggerated. It felt good to be seen as normal by someone close to me.

The madwoman within me approves of him. Somehow, she knows he accepts and believes in her. Primarily, I think this is why he is in my life, to create a home and belonging for the madwoman I carry within the crevices of my soul. I am hopeful for her development as an integrated part of society. How I will accomplish this is the challenge of my present life.

I now have a fruitful relationship with the archetype of the madwoman and her expressions in my daily life. I gained this relatedness through a Jungian approach to her. I feel great empathy with all those who struggle with mental illness, knowing how difficult it is to develop a healthy relationship with this dimension of oneself. Today, I have not yet become comfortable working with the mentally ill, seemingly because I am not yet able to differentiate this archetype in me from the one others carry. My two experiences working as a psychiatric nurse were both difficult. The first when I was a medication nurse revealed my fears of mental illness and the people who suffered with this disease. I saw myself in them. The second job resulted in me being attacked by one of my patients and this confirmed my lack of professional skillfulness in this area of nursing. Perhaps one day, I will find the ability to work well with those who suffer with this archetype. For now, the madwoman expresses herself in my artistic energy. Perhaps later in my life, she will assist in the healing of others.

At first, the decision to move to California was not easy. Ron had been born and raised in California and his parents were getting older and frail. He wanted to be near them at this time in their lives. Leaving my therapist was the biggest hurdle confronting me when we decided to move. Jason reminded me that there were Jungian therapists in California and he also offered to be available to me by phone. This was freeing to me. In considering the move, I felt I would have continuity in the transition from therapy in Louisiana to California

So Ron and I packed up on a cold January day and drove our two vehicles and one rental truck over three days to California. Ron's brother drove the truck. It was an adventure trying to stay together through cities like Phoenix. But we used walkie-talkies to stay connected. Once settled in our new home and after selling our houses in Louisiana, Ron set up his dental-smith practice, while I looked for nursing positions.

I now work as a public health nurse caring for HIV/AIDS clients. I strive to enable these clients to overcome the stigma society places on them, and to reject internalizing this stigma through self-condemnation. I know from my journey with mental illness that this is a long and painful task. I can identify with many of the struggles of my clients, who did not go out looking to get HIV, but contracted it in their search for love, life and belonging. My search for love, belonging and a place in society led me through the labyrinth of mental illness. Just their daily routine of taking medication that HIV requires allowed me to connect my responsibility for taking my psych medication to my clients' struggles. I could empathize with their fears of others finding their medications and knowing that they had HIV. Many of my clients forget or go off their meds for these reasons. I know what it is to spend a lifetime struggling with a chronic illness and its daily temptation to succumb to failure. I know that by getting up every morning and putting one foot in front of the other, one can discover a life of meaning and value. Saying yes to one's journey and creatively embracing all that is part of that journey can lead to a surprisingly beautiful outcome.

I write to gain self-expression of all that I am and have been. I am committed to the people of my everyday experiences with all my inner resources. Filled with expectation about where this kind of living will take me, I dreamed of becoming a therapist. I started graduate school to become a marriage and family therapist, and did well academically. But I left it behind because it didn't seem to fit with the journeying I had done so far. None of the classes in this therapy training were related to a Jungian approach. I have no desire to relate to mental illness in any other frame of thought because this approach has been so helpful to me. I am more attracted to studying and developing my artistic skills. This is what I pursue now.

I am planning to retire in a few years and am anticipating a new life through this change. Retirement is sort of another dying experience in my life. I have some fears related to the return of old habits like depression and mania. Yet, I have learned that these habits are part of my nature and can be embraced with skill, precision, and love. Curiosity and discovery will lead me through these dark transitions to a new expression of myself. I will always be a compassionate energy because this trait is inherent in the core of my psyche. As a wounded healer, this core will lead me to a new career for these later years of my time on this earth. I stand on tip-toe, waiting, looking, anticipating this new developing expression of me.

Perhaps, one day, my story will be a form of therapy for others by showing there is a way through darkness, something we all must encounter in different ways. And as often as the seasons change, this challenge faces us.

Chapter XII: The Divine Feminine:

In my journey with Jungian therapy and spirituality, it was the archetype of the Divine Feminine that brought the most healing for me. The surfacing of the gentle emotionally connected and courageous feminine energy within me was key to my success as a woman and a nurse. This meant I had to confront and curtail the strong, invasive, arrogant and aggressive energy of the masculine logic in Western medicine, society, my history and myself. Western Medicine labeled me mentally ill. Society saw me as a weak woman. My history trapped me as a victim. I critiqued myself as a failure. I had to learn to allow wounds to heal slowly from within without the quick solutions that so often society wants to inject.

Speaking of the Divine Feminine is beyond my verbal ability at this time in my life. I experience Her as non-verbal. She is more a presence that has streamed throughout my life. This presence started before the age of three with my fascination about my mother in that small, narrow kitchen. Mama was pregnant as she sat on a stool, creating so efficiently, nourishing meals by cleaning, sorting, cooking foods from their basic natural state. Like the Divine Feminine that creates life out of the basic materials of existence, Mama was excellent in the kitchen. The scar on my knee and Mama's comforting words from my earliest years are memories that connect me to God as Mother. My play at age nine, dancing with the wind through the pines in our yard, making flowers in the clover grass, and gazing at the stars of the Milky Way on late summer evenings were all the paths the Divine Feminine used to touch my life. The little fairy from my imagination when I was sad or frightened going to bed in the dark was Her way too of caressing me and cherishing my tears.

Once, around this age of imagination, I was taken with awe before a statue of Mary in my childhood Catholic Church. It was a youthful Mary, perhaps a tribute to her humble state at age thirteen when she became pregnant with the Divine Secret. Hidden in this young girl in a manner unacceptable at her age and in her culture was the precious womb secret that would change the world. As I gazed at the quiet motionless statue, I wondered who she was and how she would impact my little life. I became devoted, over the years, to her and the Church that tried to be like her, humble, pregnant, life changing.

My attraction to the nuns as a young adult and the imprinting I experienced in my compulsion to be with and like them were expressions of this devotion to Mary and the fruit of her womb. In the later years of my life, my relationships with other women like my sisters and girlfriends have nourished my journey with the Divine

Feminine presence that moves me emotionally. She is like music to the avid listener, the music of nature seen in flowers and the moonlit night-landscape, and stories of people as they sing their unique songs of life to the universe. The bending and bowing of trees rustled by the Santa Ana winds and hurricanes so familiar to me from my life in California and Louisiana remind me of Her power in effects yet always invisible in essence.

Lately I have come to discover this Divine Feminine energy in the Hindu story of Kali. She is the dark feminine energy in the chaos of life and death, the living cycle of destruction and creation. She hides behind every thing in my daily life experiences, peeking secretly, subtly, silently around all the corners of my existence. Her message is one of hope and love in the giving and taking away of the pleasures of life. With Her skillful hands She fills my days with sensory satisfaction found in savory food from the kitchen, stimulating work as a nurse, and vital family life with my husband, pets and friends. Yet in Her wisdom She also takes me into the desert where I must face the challenges from overindulgence in all these gifts and bear their destruction and loss. Sometimes I want and take too much and must contain my desires for these pleasures. Kali helps me with both these facets of life, the indulging and the sacrificing, the expanding and containing.

The Divine Feminine in all Her forms from various myths and religions has reached out to me especially through my wounded history and Her own story of woundedness. She is the voice in the dark of my life. She is the gentle moonlight of the unconscious that balances the often harsh daylight of conscious reality.

I was profoundly involved in the healing art of the Wounded Feminine from within my psyche as She surfaced in my dreams. The image of a cat licking her wounds and fur to bring about an inner integrity that only she understands was frequently on my mind. I had to learn to skillfully surrender to the task of the inner woman of my psyche as She sought out Her own healing in the footsteps of my life, all my life. The task of this archetype, it seems to me, is to assimilate all the suffering women have known throughout the ages. We do not readily know the wounded feminine as a collective image in our society. But it seems we, as individuals, have to give Her the space in our psyche and daily life she needs to heal herself. This task I speak of was Hers as well as mine since I too had much healing to do for my feminine self. The wounded feminine is an imprint on my psyche and on the broader psyche of humankind. This broader psyche of humankind can be called the **collective unconscious**. The image of the wounded feminine carries energy that is the result of thousands of years of neglect and abuse by the patriarchal society. This energy or archetype seeks healing through the full expression of this wound and its healing journey.

Her stories of wounding can be found in many myths of goddesses and women throughout ancient religions and cultures. I meditated on the stories of Mary in the Christian tradition and Kuan Yin and Kali in the Chinese and Hindu traditions. Mary was the mother of Jesus who silently shared in the suffering of her Son's life and death. The artwork called *The Pieta* by Michelangelo is the best expression of this wounding that I can visualize in Mary's story. But her early life of rejection for her pregnancy without marriage is another story of feminine suffering. Kuan Yin was the student of Buddha who sacrificed her step into enlightenment in order to stay behind and help others on their journeys to a better life. Kuan Yin is known as the Goddess of Compassion. Kali is an expression of the dark feminine that is connected to death and chaos, and birth and life. There are many myths of women suffering and healing themselves and their cultures but we do not commonly know them in modern times.

Meditating on these women and other stories helped put me in touch with the capacity of the feminine to be wounded and her healing journey. Her journey to wholeness and healing is fulfilled in the lives of men and women who acknowledge and respect this image of woman in the collective unconscious and in their own lives. My own images of the witch and madwoman were expressions of the dark side of this feminine archetype. I learned to see their bitterness, hatred and sometimes-violent expressions in my dreams and fantasies as coming from not only my life story but also from the wounded feminine in the collective unconscious. I find that this feminine archetype with her suffering and dark side of chaos and death has a profound healing capacity. I learned she is also very connected to the image and power of fire. Many of my paintings of the witch often involved images of fire. Fire can warm as well as destroy. It is a creative or destructive element, depending on with whom it is associated and how this energy is handled.

The Divine Feminine is a compassionate healer who lives close to the fire within my soul. This fire is the result of opposites, such as light and dark, masculine and feminine, living close together. In her book *Pregnant Darkness*, Monika Wikman speaks of this fire rising up from the dark night of the soul. I have known this dark night through my struggles with bi-polar depression and this fire burns within me. This fire surfaced for me in my first psychotic event while on the retreat. It felt like a rush of energy. My night dreams and real life have taught me that this fire can be destructive as it is in psychosis, but it also has the power to bring light and warmth to life. The fiery energy from a psychotic experience can be directed, with counseling and art therapy, into creative pursuits that lead to enlightenment and individuation. Enlightened, one can transcend suffering and desire; and individuated, one is unique and distinct from others.

Next to this fire in me, the Wounded Feminine gains the energy She needs for healing. My life became surrendered to the healing She needed through my art. Painting pictures of Her, and dialoging in loving ways with the witch and the madwoman, I discovered the beauty hidden in the Wounded Feminine. Dialoging, as I explained before, is a technique done with active imagination where an image is allowed to explain itself. Great insight into the image and what it means in one's life can be made. Just the expression of the emotions connected to the image can be very healing. The witch and madwoman revealed their hurts, which were underneath their bizarre and dysfunctional behaviors such as paranoia, delusions, and rude attacks on others.

These dialogues helped me to become empathetic with my history of mental illness, isolation and rejection. Empathy and reverence for the inner figures of the witch and madwoman revealed the vulnerable side of these negative feminine figures. Like the frog that turns into a prince with a kiss, so these images revealed in dialogue their creative, tender, nurturing natures. I soon was able to paint beautiful feminine expressions seen in mothering and wisdom figures. I meditated on the Wisdom Literature of the Bible, Sirach, Songs of Solomon, The Book of Wisdom, Psalms and Proverbs, where God was referred to as feminine. *Prayers to Sophia*, by Joyce Rupp, became my daily prayer manual. I made one painting of a ghostlike feminine figure, representing her spirit nature, as she danced with fire and flowers. I named this painting *Sophia Crowning Herself with Flowers*. This painting came from the depths of my prayer-life. I felt great warmth and love from this divine figure of God.

Having gone through this healing process with myself, I was able to gently walk, day in and day out, with my suffering patients. This allowed the Wounded Feminine within me to bring hope and comfort to others.

As a nurse, I meet with clients in the early stages of their diagnosis with HIV, when fear, shock, and shame overwhelm them. With patient, non-judgmental listening, I convey to them that they are valuable. Slowly and with repeated encounters, they begin to verbalize acceptance and hope for themselves. When clients affirm me as a caring nurse, I know it is the goddess, the Divine Feminine, within me that has brought about this emotional connection. It is the goddess and Her healing energy they are experiencing through contact with me. Once I had a client tell me I was the most compassionate woman she had ever met. I quickly helped her see that I was only a reflection of an energy and force that was within her. Simply stating, "It takes one to know one," I enabled her to see her own inner powers of compassionate, healing energy. This client eventually went on to become a caring peer advocate for others who suffer with an HIV diagnosis.

A depth of presence fills my consciousness whenever an image, symbol, or imaginative moment of the Divine Feminine crosses my mind. I would treasure the ability to share this Feminine energy with the reader. Because She is such an experiential reality rather than an intellectual or rational, verbal moment, I find it awkward to write about Her. Yet it is essential that I speak of Her as She is the healer who worked in my soul, silently, with the cover of night to bring me to the wholeness, joy and freedom I now know.

I find Her presence in my dark experiences of chaos, disillusionment, despair, failure and death. Her consoling, intangible presence when I listen to music is so sensuous, my body's pleasure confirms Her hidden reality. The cover of night, the darkness of the sea and the depth of the earth are all Her choices for embodiment and home. I am learning to embrace the suffering and chaos of my world, experiencing in this embrace, acceptance and tolerance, the gift of consolation and trust.

Lately in my transition to retirement, I find myself in the tomb of my first psychotic break with all its scary, terrifying, rotting darkness. Often, I wake in the night overwhelmed by the insecurity of change, feelings of despair and weakness. Yet in the very midst of this tomb experience, I find myself dancing, rhythmically in the sea of Her love, power and presence. Her consolation tells me She is accomplishing something wonderful in and through my suffering. My faith tells me She is creating a new wine and a new wine skin for my future. I have only to endure each day of change and its chaotic darkness with patience, restraint, and faith. The gestures of art, painting with pastels, writing poetry, or dancing with music are the tools of my endurance and the words of communion between Her irrational night sea presence and my rational response. Listening to the *Canon in D* is a moment of profound oneness between us.

In all these words, I somehow fail Her. I share my meditations in the final chapter of this book in hope of giving you, the reader, a glimpse of Her, even if only an ankle under the cloak of her dress. I pray for you to find the God of your own soul, and a relishing banquet between the two of you.

Chapter XIII: Jungian Therapy and Mental Illness

The journey through mental illness with Jungian concepts is a sacred walk filled with danger, excitement, success and failure. One is connected on this walk to the energy that creates, destroys, and vibrates in all life. A pilgrim must approach this way with awe, respect and faith. The tremendous energy we are connected to can be greater than we are able to handle without help.

This energy I speak of is contained in the symbolic forms available to us in our dreams and imagination. Dreams are our allies for getting a view into our inner natures, both positive and negative.

Dreams can be subtle and easily denied as bearing any real messages. In fact, many people live in the denial where they fail to see all their negative traits and desires suppressed just below consciousness, waiting for expression. They prefer to believe these negative aspects of themselves are controlled or absent from their personalities. This denial leads them to see their dark side expressed in others they do not like. The greater the denial, the more powerful the subconscious energy becomes.

Dreams hold the energy and teaching we need for a holistic understanding and expression of ourselves. This energy from deep within each of us and shared by all of us is the source of all we do every day, indeed of history itself.

After thirty-three years of Jungian spirituality, I have much in me that is not clear, questions not answered, problems not solved. I still struggle with the masculine energy within that is energized to seek success. I fear his potential to ignore feelings and values in my rise to the top. My story is still unfinished. I have yet to discover a clear image of the Self and how it chooses to express itself in my life. Within me, I continue to experience the vast pregnant void that yearns to become real and realized. I still seek the warmth and tenderness of the Father archetype and the nourishment of the Mother archetype. I have come to view Christ as the template of my life. I hear from my unconscious the call from Christ to "Come Out," each day wondering what that means in everyday behavior. And the intuitive warning of darkness and evil still accompanies this invitation, inviting me to be sensitive to my feelings and imagination in all my choices and behaviors. I seek in my dreams and imagination the *who* and *what* of my fate and destiny. How do I become faithful to its call and development? It is as though I am still a youth seeking my vocation and fulfilling my call to uniqueness. My insight so far is that the wounds I have known hold within them the healing they need. This message, though mysterious and unclear is what my psyche stresses most, that wounds themselves contain the healing needed, if we but search through them with help. I have learned to embrace my dark periods with love and acceptance through listening to music, painting my feelings, writing poetry and doing gestures of restorative yoga. These behaviors serve to show the negative veneer of darkness as only a cover of the dawning personal depth. Wounds serve the purpose of bringing me closer to God.

My Jungian search began in 1975 with an Ira Progoff Dialogue House workshop, which taught me how to keep a personal journal and develop my active imagination in journal writing. It gave me a concrete way of connecting to my imaginary world. This journey has continued with my daily, reflective reading of the Jungian writers most applicable to my life. I spend early morning hours in prayerful connection to my dreams and imagination. The arts of journal writing and painting are essential for my integration of the discoveries found each morning. Monthly encounters with my therapist are also part of my regular regimen for healing and wholeness. In these therapy sessions, we look at my dreams and how they express and lead me in my daily life.

My therapist helped me understand my dreams at first by teaching me to grasp what the men and women and other characters in my dreams represented. He later helped me appreciate associations I had with the many symbolic forms of my dreams by asking me questions like, "What comes to your mind with this image?" or "What do you make of this image?" He was also able to see the flow between the beginning, middle and end of the dream, and what the transitioning images were trying to get across to me. My task was mainly to write the dream down and allow him to question me about my feelings and thoughts related to its symbols and figures. Then together we would find the messages contained in each dream.

The Jungian way with mental illness requires, it seems to me, a real faith in God. God here is understood as your personal belief in a higher or greater life form than visible reality. Belief in a spiritual dimension in all life is needed to really make a Jungian pathway. In my journey, it took strong faith in this spiritual side of life to convince me that wholeness and healing awaited me, if I would just be faithful to the process.

My understanding of God has changed from a concrete father figure in the sky to belief in an evolving spiritual reality that pervades and gives birth to all aspects of our material world. I believe there are powerful forces available to us in the spiritual world, which surrounds and is within us all the time. The only way I have of truly connecting with this side of life is through my dreams, prayer-life and imagination. It is not directly available to me except through moments of synchronicity.

One example of synchronicity in my life happened the morning after I had a dream about the moon and moon people visiting the earth and engaging me. I woke confused by this dream. Then in that morning's reflections, I quite by accident opened the book, *Pregnant Darkness* by Monika Wikman. I opened the book with a random gesture to the very page where it explained the image in my dream. Here, the book spoke of the Divine transforming itself in the human soul.

Ms Wikman seemed to say that in our dreams we can discover images of the Divine, the great human being, the Anthropos. Anthropos is a term from ancient philosophy and religion that relates to the original or primal man, male or female or perhaps both. It included genetically all human individuals. This energy, figure or being still evolves today in the unconscious for the sake of the consciousness of mankind, seeking fulfillment of its own nature and story. This image in dreams may be a huge human or an extremely tiny human, "trying to find room to dwell among ordinary mortals." My dream about moon people was about the Divine transforming in my human soul. Reading the book gave me great hope and expectancy about God's moves in my life for the sake of Himself, humankind, and my tiny life too.

Later, I shared this moment of synchronicity with my therapist. It is imperative that we have a place to talk about these moments when we perceive the conscious and subconscious worlds working together. I cannot assume on my own that my evaluation of synchronicity is valid unless I get it confirmed by a trained analyst. It would be too easy for my mental illness to mislead me in these perceptions and take me into delusions or grandiose thinking.

One of the first requirements for working with a therapist is a strong desire to heal a problem. I was compelled to seek a normal life without mental illness. Today, I live a balanced emotional and practical life only because of this incessant desire within me for healing. Driven by this desire for a normal life and a place in society, I worked every day with the principles taught to me by my therapist. Today, I am in a leadership position as a public health nurse and a project director for federal grants. I am also happily married. I know this success in life because of my persistence and determination to heal using Jungian principles.

There are specific gestures we can make that serve to open and connect us to the inner life and its truths. One is reverence and responsibility for small things in daily life. When I learned the importance of closing cupboard doors I had left open, I grew in my ability to love and relate better to my husband, who was bothered by the doors left opened. Or one could simply learn to enjoy the fragrance of a flower as a gift from God. These are both examples of reverence and responsibility for small things.

Daily journaling about one's everyday life allows you to see more clearly what consumes your inner and outer activities. Some of my journal writing, in the beginning, was incoherent. I soon learned to journal mostly about the feelings and facts of my day rather than the *why's* for my behaviors. Reviewing my journal before a therapy session kept me close to my daily events so I had specific details to bring to the session.

As far as the chemical imbalance for bipolar illness, I can only say one thing. The medications will correct this imbalance. But often medication alone is not enough. Therapy is needed to heal the many wounds produced by a life with mental illness. If the psychic wounds are not healed, their destructive energy can consume your life, regardless of the type or amount of medication used. The wounds can be healed, but it takes a long time and much patience. And medication must be used to prevent the chemistry of the brain from interfering with this healing process. I continue, after twenty-eight years, to consult my therapist monthly for an hour. Wounds from forty years ago are still the topic of some sessions.

Bipolar mental illness cannot be cured with therapy alone. Just as medication alone, in my opinion, will not work. It takes one who is faithful to both a medicinal regimen and therapeutic counseling. These, coupled with disciplined solitude for one's inner life, will bring healing. I consider myself healed, but I still take a medication daily and consult my therapist monthly. I also spend at least an hour every day in solitude with my inner-world symbols and imagination.

There is loneliness in this journey that one must learn to enjoy as solitude. The gift and grace of creativity soon flood into one's everyday life and become the fruit one humbly shares with others. This book is just such a gift.

Accepting the yoke of an inner journey requires a sacrifice of some aspects of the outer journey. One's greatness is found only in the reflections of images from within, not on the faces of an adoring public. Though my journey involved many losses and failures in society, I am so grateful for the fullness of my inner world that there are no regrets for any aspects of my life. The greatest loss I feel these days is never having had children or grandchildren. Yet the vital image and energy of mother and child is strong in my nature. Even the loss of financial stability for retirement due to my limited work history during my disability for mental illness does not bring sadness into my life. I find the Jungian way of living rich with unending gifts. I could not love myself, my God, or my life anymore than I do at this time.

I have come to see mental illness in times of stress, neurosis or psychosis, as a gift or special calling in life. This calling expressed itself in my life journey as a desire to have the eyes, ears, and hands of my inner heart nature opened to experience the presence of God, Self, the Divine in everyday life. With this sensitive openness, I longed to perceive, worship, and respond to that presence with love. Often in mental illness, one is sensitive to what much of the rest of the world takes for granted. Making sense of this sensitivity is a mysterious journey, unique to each person's story. Jungian Spirituality makes that journey whole and holy.

Appendix A: Concluding Tips for a Jungian Journey with Mental Illness.

In conclusion, I want to give a few summarized tips for applying Jungian therapy to a journey with mental illness.

1. Dream-work is a central part of this therapy. Connection to dreams is one of the tasks you need to master in applying the principles of Carl Jung to the healing of mental illness. Jungian therapy is also a creative way for anyone to approach a time of transition in life, such as mid-life or old age crises. Keeping a log beside your bed is the best way to grasp these fleeting moments with the unconscious. My therapist told me that Jung once compared remembering dreams to that of trying to catch a fish with your bare hands. They are slippery, but with persistence you catch a tail, then later the body and head. This journaling can be done best as you drift off to sleep or when you wake in the night or early morning from a dream. Keep a pad and pen at your bedside for easy writing.

2. I cannot stress enough how powerful this subconscious world of reality is and how important it is to have a therapist for making sense of the sometimes confusing symbols in dreams. I believe that one who attempts to analyze his or her own dreams is like the one who attempts to go to court as his own lawyer. As a wise, anonymous person once said, "He who represents himself has a fool for a client." Because dreams are interpreted on many levels including personal, collective, archetypal and alchemical, it takes a wise, trained and objective person to look at them and find their messages. The dreamer cannot be objective with his/her own dreams. The search for a Jungian therapist is challenging but possible with the help of the Internet and talking with reputable therapists in your area for recommendations. One of the first requirements for working with a therapist is a strong desire to heal

a problem. The Jungian therapist you choose should be able to teach and guide you through the concepts, archetypes and myths that are part of your personal make-up. Your regular meetings with this therapist will reveal to him/her the issues most relevant to your healing process. One can seek out a therapist long before insanity challenges existence. Perhaps one significant dream is all you need to get started. But the desire to know what lies beneath all you perceive with your five senses is a requirement for this endeavor. Then a mixture of grace, commitment and imagination will connect you to the archetypes and myths that hold the most meaning for you.

3. Dream analysis is a part of almost every session but connection to your conscious reality of everyday living must not be neglected. The subconscious journey and daily reality go hand and hand. It takes close attention to both in order to make sense of either dimension. Keep a journal of your daily activities and related feelings. Daydreaming and fantasies that come to us at varying moments in our day are worth remembering. Jotting them down in the moment for later reflection keeps one from wandering in the fantasy while living the details of life. This takes a playful yet respectful awareness of our flow of imagination. In your daily notebook, in a separate section, keep a log of these fantasies and memories that come to mind, particularly repeating images from your life and imagination.

4. Set a specific time for journaling and active imagining. When not in these specific time periods, focus your attention on reality and your responsibilities in relation to it. In other words, keep your conscious and unconscious worlds separate with a definite boundary between the two. We should impose boundaries on our subconscious expressions. We must view the subconscious with awe and respect, but we must set limits on it too. As my therapist taught me, we should have a small ego that is very strong. We

need to be small before the reality of the unconscious but strong in constructively relating to it. There needs to be limits on what our imagination and fantasies can suggest to us. I once heard from a friend about a relative who had an anger management problem. The relative kept a sign in his vehicle that said, "Don't get out of the truck." This could have been his way of setting a boundary for his inner world when overcome with road rage. I did not learn to use discipline and a boundary for the unconscious energies from my dreams and imaginary dialogues until it was almost too late, as evidenced by my attempted suicide after dialoging with the inner figure, Hermes. I had repeated failures in relating positively to feelings and thoughts from my subconscious. I grew tired of the wrecked life I was leading by allowing my dark side full expression in mania and depression. I had to choose to limit this inner world's expression in my daily life. I began focusing more on keeping a job and being a successful nurse. This brought balance to my inner and outer worlds. When you do sense a strong connection between your conscious and unconscious dimensions, journal about it and discuss it with your therapist rather than try to analyze or act on this awareness. Try to develop a healing relationship and attitude towards the feelings, thoughts, and awareness you have from your deeper self.

5. Keep a separate notebook for notes from the practice of meditation and active imagining. Find a meditation practice that is natural for you in which you relax and allow your images and feelings to move spontaneously without judgment. Yoga, listening to music, dance, singing, drawing and painting, or reading poetry are just a few of the avenues for opening up the imagination. Keep notes on the thoughts and feelings these practices bring up. Bring your images from dreams, fantasies, and memories to this practice. Allow yourself to relate to these images without critical evaluation. This skill requires you consciously engage in an

almost playful, imaginary dialogue with the image. This should be done at a specific time of solitude set aside for this purpose. My favorite time of day for active imagining is early morning after waking from the dream world. I do this best if I paint or draw the image as I attempt to relate to it. The quality of this art is not for a critical eye. It is done simply for the sake of expression and is not to be judged for its artistic merit. This method often brought out feelings and values connected to the image, which I then took back into my therapy sessions. The more you engage a symbolic expression from dreams with artistic encounters, the more the symbol comes to life for you. This helps you understand its specific purpose for being in your unconscious.

6. Take a thread of continuity found in your dreams, daily life, memories, fantasies, and active imagination to your therapist to talk about on a regular basis. In the early stages of my therapy, I worked sometimes as often as twice a week with my therapist. You and the therapist will decide how often encounters are necessary. Your therapist may also suggest reading that is related to your particular journey. Finding Jungian authors whose style of writing you can grasp and emotionally relate to is important. My therapist often suggested Jungian books that would help me along the way, but he cautioned me to read them with my feeling-self, rather than my logical, critical mind. He seemed to know that only certain aspects of a book would apply to me. It was my job to discover a feeling-connection to each Jungian concept to which I was introduced. It isn't necessary to understand all concepts; only the ones that directly touch your own experience are needed. I did read some books, which were over my head and didn't make sense to me, but finding the nuggets of gold where I connected on a feeling level made the task worthwhile.

Finally, it is my hope that my life story will encourage you to search through the dark periods in your own life. May you discover all that waits for you in the realm of the subconscious you encounter knowingly and unknowingly every day. Take heed of those fleeting thoughts and vague dreams, which you may easily dismiss as unimportant daydreaming. Keep in your journal those repeating behaviors you just can't stop. Here, you may find the hidden desires of your life and the energy you need to fulfill those dreams. Here, you may find the healing for all the brokenness you may have known. I cannot prescribe that you begin a Jungian journey. But if you have similar feelings and wounds as I, perhaps along with your psychiatrist and medications, you could seek out a Jungian therapist and begin a Jungian spirituality for deeper healing. If you do not have a mental illness, but experience wounding from all life's demands, you too could begin this form of spirituality in order to enhance meaning and uniqueness for your own life story.

Appendix B: Reference Books and Recommended Reading

<u>In Midlife, A Jungian Perspective</u>, Murray Stein, Spring Publication, Inc., Dallas Texas, 1983. This book is particularly helpful when encountering a transition time in life such as mid-life and old age crises. It explains the archetype of Hermes as companion energy for the transition.

<u>On Dreams and Death, A Jungian Interpretation</u>, Marie-Louise von Franz, Shambhala, Boston and London, 1987. This book brings awareness to the place of dream symbols in the death or dying transitions in life.

<u>Mid-life Spirituality and Jungian Archetypes</u>, Janice Brewi, and Anne Brennan, NICHOLAS-HAYS Inc., York Beach, Maine, 1999. This text is a simply written introduction to Jungian concepts in mid-life time.

<u>The Far Side of Madness</u>, John Weir Perry, Spring Publication, Inc., Dallas Texas, 1974. Though Perry's writings are challenging for me to read and comprehend, he expresses strong insight to the processing of psychosis as a transformative experience in one's life.

<u>Pregnant Darkness, Alchemy and Rebirth of Consciousness</u>, Monika Wikman, NICOLAS-HAYS, Inc., Berwick, Maine 2004. A beautifully written, meditative type book on the transforming process understood through the stages of alchemical theory.

<u>Light From the Darkness, The Paintings of Peter Birkhauser</u>, BirkhauserVerlag, Basel. Boston. Stuttgart, 1980. This collection of art by Peter is a view into how one can use art to process the mysterious images from the unconscious without losing their power and energy. His painting skills are excellent and he gives one an impression of the profound energy contained in the personal and collective unconscious.

Prayers to Sophia, A companion to The Star In My Heart, Joyce Rupp, Innisfree Press, Inc., 2000. I used this collection of prayer-type poems as a daily prayer manual.

The Progoff Intensive Journal Program for Self Development, 800-221-5844 info@intensivejournal.org. This web site is worth checking out as a possible resource for learning to use a journal to apply Jungian concepts to one's everyday life.

Pathways to Bliss, Mythology and Personal Transformation, Joseph Campbell, Joseph Campbell Foundation, New World Library, Novato, Ca. 2004. This is another meditative read on thoughts about the Self and self-understanding.

Thou Art That, Transforming Religious Metaphors, Joseph Campbell, Joseph Campbell Foundation, New World Library, Novato, Ca. 2001.This manuscript is for meditative reflecting on the religious function of the psyche and the development of self.

Reflections on the Art of Living: A Joseph Campbell Companion, Selected and edited by Diane K Osbon, Harper Perennial, 1991. This is a collection of meditative thoughts that deepen one's experience of life.

The Pregnant Virgin, A Process of Psychological Transformation, Marion Woodman, Inner City Books, Toronto, Canada, 1985. This is an insightful writing on the archetype of the pregnant virgin and the process of individuation. The images of the pregnant virgin were often in my art and lead me to read this book. It opened me to the power of symbol to assist in changing one's self-expression.

The Power Of Myth, with Bill Moyers, Joseph Campbell, Betty Sue Flowers, Editor, Broadway Books, New York, 1988. This is a series of interviews of Joseph Campbell by Bill Moyers that helps one develop a personal philosophy and open approach to religious myths.

For Women Growing Older, The Animus, Jane Hollister Wheelwright, C.G. Jung Educational Center of Houston, Texas Inc, 1984.This is a brief insight to the development of the masculine principle in women and in the collective unconscious of our day.

The Soul's Code, In Search of Character and Calling, James Hillman, Warner Books Edition, New York, NY, 1996. This book is an invitation to learn how to view the Self and your unique journey with your destiny or fate.

Encarta World English Dictionary, Bloomsbury Publishing Plc 1999. An excellent resource for understanding the unfamiliar words used by Jungian authors. Often these are words not used in everyday conversation and need to be understood in the context of the writing. This dictionary helped me process many terms.

Care of the Soul, Thomas Moore, Harper Perennial, New York, New York, 1994. Though this maybe a challenging read for the non-spiritual person, it helps one appreciate the innate religious function of the psyche. It assists one in developing a spiritual approach to life.

Psychology and Alchemy, CG Jung, The Collected Works of CG Jung, Vol 12, translated by R. F. C. Hull, Second Edition, Bollengen Series XX, Princeton University Press. This is an in-depth study of the interrelationship of dreams, transformation of the psyche, and alchemical philosophy. It contains many gold nuggets and images for meditation. It helped me appreciate my journey in the development of a personal philosophy and religious views for life.

Appendix C: Reference Glossary:

Active Imagination: a meditative processes whereby a person engages an image from a dream or fantasy or personal history. In this meditative encounter, one employs functions other than rational thought, such as painting, dance, yoga, meditation prayer or other form of meditative practice, which allows images and imagination to develop spontaneously. The purpose of this practice is to engage the image subject so that it unfolds its meaning, purpose, or message.

Alchemy (Alchemical): originally, as the predecessor of chemistry and modern science, it was an early unscientific form of chemistry that sought to transform base medals into gold and discover the life-prolonging elixir or a universal cure for disease. Alchemy as a part of Jungian psychology is connected to the philosophy of alchemy that came from the study of symbols in religions and myths. It concerns itself with the transforming of base aspects of the personality into higher, purified expressions, the gold of the personality and life. It is a symbolic way of viewing and encountering the depth of psychic change and transformations. Further study of this complex subject is needed to fully understand it by the average person. (From the Encarta Dictionary and personal reflections.)

Anima: the female principle in the male psyche. It is manifested predominately in images of women in dreams and fantasies.

Animus: the male principle in a female psyche. It is manifested predominately in images of men in dreams and fantasies.

Archetype: an image from the collective unconscious in Jungian psychology, an inherited memory represented in the mind by a universal symbol and observed in dreams and myths. We meet archetypal images in the universals of myth, religion, legend, fairytales, and folklore. An example of archetype is the divine child, or the hero, or the mother, and so on. (From the Encarta Dictionary and personal reflections.)

Bi-polar mental illness: an affective disorder in which a person has emotional episodes of highs and lows, mania and depression. Also known as manic-depressive illness.

Carl Jung: a Swiss psychiatrist who broadened Freud's interpretation of the unconscious. He introduced the concepts such as introvert and extrovert. He developed an understanding of the collective unconscious and all its opposing energies and archetypes. (Encarta Dictionary and personal reflections.)

Collective Unconscious: the inherited part of the unconscious thought, memory or instinct, which is common to members of a people and is observable through dreams and behaviors. (Encarta Dictionary)

Complex: a group of images or ideas held together by a common emotional tone. Complexes are an individual matter, but at the bottom of each complex lay an archetype or archetypal image. (From Jane Hollister Wheelwright's book, For Women Growing Older, The Animus.)

Dark side of God: the unfathomed, unknown dimensions of God, the invisible and inexpressible facets of God.

Depth Psychology: the study of the mind and mental states from the perspective of Carl Jung, Sigmund Freud and others. Depth psychology seeks to explore underlying motives as an approach to various mental disorders with the belief that uncovering these motives is intrinsically healing.

Dialogue: a technique in which imaginary conversation is used between oneself and a symbol from a dream or fantasy. This dialogue should be spontaneous and free of conscious rationalization as to what words the dialogue should contain. It is imaginary and done in a meditative state.

Differentiation: a task of the masculine side of the personality that aims to separate facts and values and feelings contained in a situation in order to have a clear insight for the sake of choices to be made.

Divine Child: as an archetype or image from the unconscious, it is the child with a god-like nature. The child often has powers and abilities beyond the appropriated skills for its age. It is sometimes an image of the Self. (Personal reflections)

Divine Feminine: an archetype that reveals God as feminine and in such roles as the Great Mother, Sophia and other feminine goddesses from throughout history

Dream work: a process for gaining insight into the meaning and messages from the unconscious in a dream. It should be done with the dreamer and a therapist discussing the symbols in the dream and the flow of the dream from one event or image to another.

Hermes: in Greek mythology, the messenger of the gods and son of Zeus. Hermes is the patron of athletes, thieves, and trade and was depicted with wings on his cap and sandals. He is credited with the invention of the harp.

Hypomania: a feeling of intense energy that leads to creative ideas and actions. Can be a stage just before a true manic episode in a bi-polar person. Manic episodes are different in that in mania one is out of control with excessive busy actions and thoughts that are not productive and more like chaos than creativity.

Ira Progoff: an American psychotherapist, 8-2-1921 to 1-1-1998, best known for his development of the Intensive Journal Method while at Drew University. His main interest was in depth psychology and particularly the humanistic adaptation of Jungian ideas to the lives of ordinary people. He founded Dialogue House in New York City to help promote his method. (Encarta Dictionary)

Individuation: a process of psychological development in Jungian psychology. It is the process of developing the self. One is challenged to resolve the conflicts arising at life's transitional stages such as adolescents to adulthood, adult middle life or old age. At each transition one becomes more complete and expressive of these unique developments of the Self. (Encarta Dictionary and personal reflections.)

Minotaur: a Greek myth of a monster with the body of a man and head of a bull that lived in the Cretan labyrinth and was fed human sacrifices until Theseus killed it. It was the lover of Theseus who gave him the key to his success in killing the Minotaur. She gave Theseus a ball of yarn so he could track his way into and out of the labyrinth, something no one before him was able to do. (Encarta Dictionary and further personal study of the myth.)

Myth: an ancient story. A traditional story about heroes and supernatural beings, often explaining the origin of natural phenomena or aspects of human behavior. (Encarta Dictionary)

Neuroses: a mild psychiatric disorder characterized by anxiety, depression, and possibly hypochondria. (Encarta Dictionary)

Night sea journey: a term referring to the task of fulfilling the inner call of one's life through connection to the unconscious journey we make from birth to death. It is about integrating all one's strengths and weaknesses and discovery of the Self. It often starts with a crisis or at a transition stage in development.

174

Persephone: in Greek mythology, the daughter of Demeter and Zeus. Hades, king of the underworld, abducted her. She spent half of the year in the underworld and half of the year on earth with her mother. Her return to earth is symbolized in the arrival of spring.

Primary Material: the raw or basic facets or material of the personality that has not yet been transformed in the individuation process. It would be the raw material submitted to the philosophical symbolic processes in the alchemical transformation of the personality. This raw material would be transformed into the gold or elixir of life or the Self that the individuation process seeks.

Projection: a mental process in which one focuses inner material on an outer event or individual. (Jane Hollister Wheelwright's book, For Women Growing Older: The Animus).

Psyche: human spirit or soul, encompassing the human mind as center of thought and behavior.

Self: the organizing principle of the psyche. It is an archetype of wholeness that is beyond the consciousness of the individual. It is experienced as beyond the personal or broader than the individual consciousness of self. (Personal reflections from Jane Wheelwright's book, For Women Growing Older: The Animus.)

Shadow: the unconscious part of the personality, which the conscious ego tends to ignore or reject. It is personified in dreams as persons of the same sex as the dreamer. Though unconscious to us, it may be quite obvious to others. Sometimes it can be that the archetype represents sexual and aggressive instincts inherited from a more primitive stage of humanity. (Jane Hollister Wheelwright's book, For Women Growing Older: The Animus, and Encarta Dictionary, and personal reflections.)

Soul: the non-physical aspect of a person, the complex of human attributes that manifests as consciousness, thought, feeling and will, regarded as distinct from the physical body. Soul for me is that place in our make up where we partner with God. I use psyche and soul interchangeably.

Splits with reality: involves a conscious behavior that a person performs or a conscious thought process that is somehow broken off or separated from its true origin or source in the unconscious. Rather than the consciousness of the individual operating with an awareness of the unconscious energy, the two are broken off and divided from awareness.(Personal reflections)

Subconscious: that which exists but is unknown in the conscious mind. Mental activity not directly perceived by consciousness, from which memories, feelings, or thoughts can influence behavior without the person realizing it.(Encarta Dictionary)

Synchronicity: a co-incidence of events that seem related but are not obviously caused one by the other. The events seem to be from the encounter of mutual energy waves from the conscious and unconscious worlds, acting together, ultimately exposing and emphasizing the other. (Encarta Dictionary and personal reflections.)

Unconscious: the mind's hidden part, the part of the mind containing memories, thoughts, feelings and ideas that the person is not generally aware of but that manifest themselves in dreams and dissociated acts. I use subconscious and unconscious interchangeably. (Encarta Dictionary)

Wounded Feminine: an archetype of the feminine energy that has been abused, violated or abandoned by individual, culture, or historic developments. Sometimes it is associated with this image is the witch or madwoman. (Personal reflections.)

Witch or Madwoman: an image of the wounded feminine that has a psychiatric disorder and/or has magical or wonderworking powers that can be used kindly or malevolently. (Encarta Dictionary and personal reflections.)

Meditations by Patty

Dawn and Dusk
If Only I Could Surf
Just Before Dawn
Painful Throat
Vacancy
Vacancy Revisited
Somewhere Within Me
Scorching Heat Of No Love
The Adventure
Sophia, My Inspiration for Art
Vespers
Discipleship
Mother Divine
Flaming Red Lit with Fire
Second Birthing
Waves of Joy
Treasures

Dawn and Dusk

Dawn and I are friends,
faithful and consistent.
I am tree at the shoreline of night meeting day,
colored, rising sun
peeking at the horizon.
Naked, I am firmly rooted
in the soil of this sanctuary,
trunk and roots poised in firm, delicate balance.
Responsive to the flow of Breath
blowing through my flesh and hollow mind.
My soul dancing in, through,
all around me.
Together with emptied, open mind
we worship, surrender, bond,
the beginning of a new day.

Dusk is another story.
Body and mind needy,
exhausted, poured out,
hungry beyond belief.
Where do I go to find home,
pose of love, understanding, laughter?

I am infant, orphan
helplessly small and incapable.
Where is the knock on my door,
promise of the Divine Father
to hold, heal and nourish its young?

Do I lack the sense for His presence
as though without nose or mouth, eyes or ears?
Or has He really failed to show,
abandoning His offspring?

What am I to do with this emptiness, helplessness?
Waiting without action seems impossible.
Hunger's restless energy compels.
Body, soul, mind tense with desire
without a still point of balance.

When will He come?
I knock on His door
at the darkening of day
with prayer, art, music, dance,
desperate in active waiting.
My whole existence eaten from within,
as the beast of instinct devours
with the passion for food, master
father, lover.
Convinced of His reality and power
yet longing for poise, security, purpose,
gift of soul's primacy in fleshy life.

Little did I know of God's and my father's brokenness,
need for grounding in the flesh of expression.
His wound tangled in my flesh,
needing my massage and care,
touching his wound at head and shoulders,
disconnect of mind and body.
He, source of all healing humor,
unable to belly-laugh.

I wait at Dusk,
end of day, final vision,
crying infant, orphan,
kneading my own flesh,
baking the bread of my life
in the fire of my hungry soul,
waiting for His laughter,

His roar, tickling my being
feeding, freeing me with spasms of joy.

If Only I Could Surf

If only I could learn,
waiting with breathing,
like the surfer's skill
amidst swelling waves and undercurrents.

Waiting,
breathing in the moment,
feeling power in the surge,
an ocean wave.
Complex, hidden currents,
below.

Repeating,
restless,
nagging moments,
like ocean waves,
compulsion's urges to move
without conviction, direction.

Empty moments,
confronted by wave's choices,
compel,
consume.
Wandering action without reflection,
stumbling, falling,
mistaken choices
without consideration of options.

Wait, breathe.
Breathe deep
with the belly's ocean.
Feel the energy of the urge,
to and fro impulses,
finding balance.

Flexing the muscles,
letting the ankles do the work,
grounding to the surf's board,
body board, strong, connected.
Power of an addiction's wave
engaged with mind and body.

Compulsive urge
without poise,
or breathing still point,
leads to separation of body, mind, and soul.
Giving into dark, instinctual energy,
without breath and being,
urge toppling the flesh,
into the chaos of the sea,
overcome with compulsion's force.

Feeling the swell
undefined, unconscious,
waves rising
up into the flesh,
wanting resolution now.
Stopped
for a moment
with breath, being, poise.
Pause and impulse together,
soul and body together.
Finding direction.
Safely, riding wave into gesture,
shoreline of choice expression.

Just Before Dawn

Before the day-breeze rises,
before shadows flee,
at the darkest moment of the night,
just before dawn,
come, walk with me.
Walk in me.

In a gesture of stillness and a moment of solitude,
with precision and skill, embrace me.
Put to usefulness
the restlessness that haunts me,
drives me into wandering.

In my soul where there is no matter,
be what matters most to me.
Let my matter, my flesh,
my gestures of busyness
become real extensions of your fruitfulness,
the fruitfulness of our union.

It is beyond my knowing,
this moment you touch my soul,
like the forgetfulness of the infant
for life before birth,
the mother of her labor pains
with her offspring in her arms.

This fleeting reality of spirit and matter,
at one in the place I dwell from,
center of my being,
is known only in the aftermath of its touching.
Split second though it may be,
even, at times, only a gesture

of longing and intent
like the fingers of God and man,
reaching, touching
this moment of touch,
this gesture of desire
the essence of all living,
remains the purpose of my life:
to live in the energy between us.

I will seek out the stillness of life
at the dawning of light,
knowing night,
the reflective background of the light,
is the requirement for light's emergence.

I will accept the unknowing
of this moment of transition,
the blindness I must endure
in my walk with you,
for which I long the most.

You are the breath within me,
the morning breeze when shadows flee,
I discover that I am loved,
cherished by the Light of Day,
energized by the shadows and the sun.

Painful Throat

It hurts to hurt.
Who are you, Pain?
How I long to feel and un-feel you.

Throat, tight with tension.
Vocal cords un-tuned, untamed,
hungry and thirsty for righteousness,
right order, everything in its place,
peace and poise.

Fear overwhelms,
fear of hearing my own voice,
its notes out there,
painfully different and alone.
No audience of reception.

Come Pain, let your hands
calloused from hard work,
strong from inheritance,
tune my vocal cords,
strike them to release
the music meant to come
from and through them.

Painful Feelings, soothe these tight cords
with your tears of compassion.
Let your rough-grained fingerprints
tweak and make them responsive
to the breath that flows in and out.

Hurtful Moments, strum my instrument,
 releasing the music of my soul,
wordless music,
gratefully raw and unredeemed music,
filling the air with my notes,
hanging on trees,

bonding with the earth,
soaking into the soil of a listening audience,
tilling,
soothing,
seeding,
flourishing,
finding redemption.

Vacancy

There is a nagging vacancy in me,
an emptiness that I remember feeling as a small child.
I related to it then with painful, hopeful longing.
Then it was like a hole in my heart that had a unique shape
which someday would be filled by my discovery of something or someone
having the same shape as it,
fitting like the missing piece of a puzzle.

This nagging vacancy has driven
everything I have ever done,
all the choices of my life.
Its energy and empty vibrancy causes a restlessness,
wandering like two lions seeking something to devour,
to fill the emptiness, to satiate the hunger.

This vibrating hole in my heart and the loneliness,
uniqueness, hunger, rejection
marking its existence,
motivates my compassionate energy.
Endless compassion, beyond my ego willfulness.
This black hole,
center of all my efforts to touch others,
sees itself in the wounded, broken,
dis-heartened people of my life.
With every beat of my heart,
it reaches out for one like itself.

I look, pray and search every day
for the missing puzzle piece.
Where is the completeness, integrity,
fulfillment to who I am?
It seems I am at the end of my rope
seeking the something or someone
right for this nagging, vibrating vacancy.
Shrinking from existence and relatedness,
shrinking into this hole,

living in its tears, blackness, longing,
discovering that it is beyond definition or boundary,
giving no clue to its compliment,
its mate or matching piece.
I suppose there is no matching piece.

Can I learn to exist in this negative, empty space?
Can I experience a relatedness to it,
allowing me and it to know peace, separate yet together?
I fear not
for its energy is such a still, motionless power
It feels like death, decay, dissolution.
My tears take me there for moments of deep intimacy,
but I cannot stay there to complete existence.
Its no-whereness and nothingness brings me
to a complete stop and end.
I must get up and out of it,
its nagging never leaves me alone.
Thank God for the duties of reality.
And when there are no duties,
there is always food,
addiction that possess me.
God have mercy on me.

Vacancy Revisited

Now, I ask again,
what of this hole in my heart
that nags me for attention?
I cannot ignore it with busyness
or cover it with food to satiate its dark hunger.

It is as though a fleshy wound,
a pierced slit of open flesh,
capable of stretching to accommodate any visitor.
Opening wide to its dark depth,
a depth beyond what the mind can comprehend.

Only music can pierce its darkness,
loneliness, painful longing.
Music and tears bring me to stretch my flesh
over this wound,
like a template of who I am and will become.
The hole now a window with skin stretched thin
to transparency.
It is my body that longs
to taste this pleasure of connection to the soul of me.

The negative veneer of darkness gives way,
in these moments of musical intimacy,
to the dawning of new personal awareness and insight,
to the I AM of my deepest being,
the I Will Become All You Become,
motivating my efforts to grow beyond,
beyond yet through the woundedness of my life.

And so, the Head must go,
get up and out
of this space with nagging intimacy.
Intellect, Logic,
The Rational can only play the fool,
who wants to build three tents
of permanency, concreteness and home,

in this sanctuary of transcendence,
where, for a moment,
hole and heart,
wound and spear,
body and soul
become one ambient light,
dark knowing of acceptance, love.

I have come to know You,
the dark You that is at the core of my life.
Your presence never leaves me.
Your absence is your presence.
Your vast vacancy is a fullness,
aching, painful as it is.
It is my dearest friend,
Secret, mysterious,
without words of connection.
For your language is ancient,
strange to the modern mind,
undecipherable yet powerful, piercing.

My flesh knows you well,
having born your absence since its earliest age.
Your strange verbiage of feed me,
be fed by me,
haunts the flesh,
teases it,
brings it to its knees
of worship and awe.

My mind surrenders
to the Yes
You give in Your longing for my fleshy existence,
to the Yes
of the body's urges for validation of its oneness with You..

There is actually a We in all of this,
My heart is heavy with this We,
full and empty,

hear and not here..
My body stands on tiptoe,
waiting, expecting,
tasting in its hunger
the Coming your absence promises.

.

Somewhere Within Me
Be still my soul!

Crying, angry, overwhelmed infant,
 sucking hard and frantically at the mother's breast,
 needing her warmth and tender flesh,
 gaze of her eyes to calm the restless one.

Where?
Where is the emotional sustenance of my life?
These days, mostly evenings,
overwhelmed,
emotional and physical impact of passionate living
goes by without notice of another.

If Andy were here, he would say,
"Let's go down to the pier,
watch the ships come into port
in the dark of this night."
There we would talk,
dream of better days.
Stories of passions fulfilled,
unique expressions.
We would find voice for our life's desires,
infinite capacities of soul,
finite dimensions of body.

Somehow in this night by the water,
quiet ships slipping into harbor,
we would find peace,
a peace that would allow completion.
Exhaustion and restlessness
combining in harmony and resolution.
Filled with this peaceful encounter
with friend and water,
silently moving ships in the dark,

we went our separate ways,
content with ourselves again
ready for sleep and a new day.

Andy is no longer here,
I am alone,
longing for an intimacy of embrace
of who and what i am,
without judgment,
filled with hope and anticipation
of where my soul is heading.
Someone to carry me across the canyons of my life
where exhaustion and restlessness haunt me.
Someone to still my soul:
a mother, a father, a brother or sister,
a friend,
a lover of canyons,
and its energy,
filling in empty spaces.

My need for help is desperate
as I white-knuckle my way
through the canyon spaces of empty evenings.
Anger at the absence of emotional support
consumes my body with spasms of aggression
to the empty air all around me.
When the aggressions subside,
there is only me
empty space of evening,
still waiting for the words,
flesh,
comfort of the breast.

Be still my soul,
God is near.
Find your nourishment in Her,

in Her absence.
Somehow, somewhere,
She is here,
without me seeing or feeling
somewhere within me,
She is here.

Scorching Heat of No Love

Flowers, red, yellow, pink, and purple
bloom in the garden of my soul
the soil of my being.
Craving, reaching, absorbing
light and water,
seeds waiting in timeless moments
for unfolding beauty
to reveal and achieve their purpose.

Scorching summer heat
dawn to dusk
saps away all hope of life and beauty.
Scorching sun of logic without love
bright, powerful, unyielding.
Searching focus of critique and condemnation.
Fragile life, not meant for this pointed discernment,
like an infant without the swaddling embrace of mother.

Winter and Summer rains of mothering nourishment
from above and deep into the soil
are never enough to overcome
constant harsh light's power.
Delicate revelations of endlessly up-reaching,
rooting-roots
dry, limp, burnt in scorching heat.
Some plants give up and die,
some struggle to live with wilted stems and sagging leaves.
Weeds seem to flourish
in the heat of illumination without love.

Where is the shade for those of us,
delicate, not meant to be sun plants?
How do we find the shade
that allows
gentle morning sunlight,
filtered high-noon brilliance,
softening heat of setting sun?

Where is the man who works with his woman
to parent the child with sun and rain
into a unique flourishing story,
The man and woman who together
produce gentle, fluid light
for their young to become?

Can I provide shade
from my searching intellect?
Can I center
soaking in my soul's environment
maturing seeds of new life?

I Choose
gentle morning sun
while the moon still shines
low in the Western sky
feeding my inner being with music and meditation.

I Choose
hiding
in the shade of the quiet, indiscernible
discernment of my body's organs
as I encounter the noonday sun of daily work.

I Choose
resting
in the reflective moon light
of early evening
as the sun slowly
surrenders to the darkening day.

I Flourish
when Sun and Moon,
rain and shine,
heart and mind
love and logic
reign together.

Equal in power and presence
mutually bowing in recognition
and need of the other
for the sake of blossoming, new life.

The Adventure

I had a dream the other night.
In this dream,
I had the ability to place my hands on my chest,
open my ribcage,
expose my beating heart.
What an image!
Power.
Gesture.
What an Adventure!

Mystical, symbolic image of openness,
availability,
readiness,
profoundly frightening,
inviting.

No longer closed
or locked, but
allowing people and things
passing through my heart,
freely?

Heart, center of my emotional being,
center of what I value most in life.
With this gesture of openness,
my heart becomes frank and
honest,
receptive,
public,
vulnerable.

Can I be so vulnerable,
allowing access to the inside,
not sealed over,
apart and wide,

transparent,
receptive,
ready and willing to accept and listen?
This would require
that I become so focused
on the incoming event
that no distractions are possible.

My heart would be like an open countryside
with no boundaries,
no fences
to block or stifle passage,
freely accessible to all,
with no restrictions on entry,
membership
or acceptance.

This openness implies a vacancy,
where I am ready and available for visitors,
applicants,
perhaps even dwellers.
Vacancy implies emptiness,
waiting to be filled.
Even a willingness
to endure loneliness,
judgment,
rejection,
all the while waiting,
openly.

Vacancy, emptiness,
must be switched on,
keenly perceptive,
ready to respond
to the presence of one
who chooses to enter
through the open door,

the open ribcage,
to touch the exposed heart.

Sharply alert,
I would focus all my attention
on the incoming relationship,
my whole body,
eyes and ears
ready to respond.
An open hand to parallel
this generous heart
that chooses to expose itself
to all the wonders of the world.

How can I do all this?
I, who have known in the past
such dark hurt to this heart.
This heart, closed
hidden within my chest,
protected from use and abuse.

As the saying goes,
"I will learn to sing a song
to the dawn
at midnight!"
I will choose to live
believing
that all life is a spiritual adventure,
darkness, a precursor to dawn
hurt, a transitional stage to fulfillment.

Open heart,
detached from both desire and fear.
Allowing spiritual adventure,
life through death,
birth from the womb,

union of opposites,
adventure of love.

Sophia, My Inspiration for Art
Prayer to Divine Wisdom, Feminine Side of God.

Sophia,
I see You on the canvas,
in the canvas of my life.
Secretly, ghost-like,
You dance the fire of intuition,
canvas of dark colors
mixed with highlights of flesh tones.

It is the dance of my life
my deepest self,
a feminine presence of the exquisite,
the vulnerable,
strength and creativity.
It is a dance before,
energized by,
a feminine Deity.
I am called to worship and adore
her moon-lit beauty.

Sometimes I feel fear,
shame in letting this Woman out,
fear that her excitement and shameless joy
over her own image will go too far,
become a rude spectacle of raw,
passionate,
innocent nudity.

Yet, I stand defiant
in the beating Sun
of human greed, carelessness and critical judgments.

I will let Her out,
celebrate Her glory
that has no marked birth or death to define Her.

Sophia's effectiveness is behind the scenes of life,
found in the mediocre and ordinary
binding wounded humanity together.
It is the bigness of littleness,
the greatness of humble life,
beauty of the familiar and routine
bringing healing and wholeness to the broken soul.

I long to hear the music
that fills your silent flesh with dance,
celebration,
the music that fills my sagging flesh
you choose to possess.

Giving vent to the You
I sense with all my senses
is what gives meaning to my life.
I bow to Your healing plan,
letting woundedness be the truth I speak.
Let me live with passion and courage
Your simple message of shameless joy
as You crown Yourself with flowers,
allowing us,
caught in time,
to touch the velvet petals
that fall from Your eternal, creative process.

Vespers

Did you ever see a flower as its petals were unfolding,
revealing in this moment
its first and final purpose before it dies?
Does the flower know my recognition
of its fleeting expression of eternal beauty?
Does it care that I care?
Do our eyes meet in a moment of mutual recognition
as we pass?

There is a delicateness of life in these moments.
Reminds me of the fine line between life and death.
How many moments in my day are like the flower,
revelations of my first and final purpose,
unfolding finite expressions of eternal beauty.
Tonight I pray to cherish the revelations of life
in the routine and ordinary
that will never come my way again.

What I know of the evening
is the slowing down,
the letting go,
the long desired rest,
the coming home and the dying of the day.
Why can't I transition well from day to night,
from life to death,
like the flower that gently bows its head
to its wilting and dissolution?

Instead, at Vespers time,
I am restless
want sleep to come
without my conscious preparation and participation.
This is the dark side of the life-death-life cycle,
hardest for me,
when darkness takes over the light of day,
when light bows its head to the yoke of the dark,
dominance by night's unknowing.

Is there a connection
between the daily failures of the arrogant and powerful ego
to notice this bowing of light to dark?
Does life take on the yoke of death for reason and purpose?

As I approach the surrender of day to night,
let my restlessness over unfinished tasks,
goals, and aspirations
give way to reverence
for the power and purpose of death and dying.
Let my arrogance that perceives life
only from my point of view,
holds so tightly to my way,
give way to the powerless position of reverence.
Enable me to take on rituals of preparation,
surrender that make the sacredness of evening
real in my life.

May I learn to relinquish with peace,
integrity, and right order
my own conscious control over life and responsibility.
May I do this each evening
as a preparation for my final days and ultimate end.

May rest come easily to me each evening
with my willful yes to the brevity,
insignificance of my existence.

May every gesture I make in preparation for sleep
be an act of faith in the Dark Side of God,
the purpose of my unknowing.
For allowing this mystery of darkness,
its reasoning,
to take hold of my evenings and nights
will surely lead me to the gentle embrace of death,
my final resting place,
refreshment.

Discipleship

"She entered the soul of a servant of the Lord, and withstood fearsome kings with signs and wonders." Wisdom 10:16

Just your position as I AM makes you a fearsome king.
I do not know what you want.
I do know that my heart and flesh is yours for the asking.
My ego,
the I am that I am,
must learn to serve this purpose,
this way of living,
where all that exists within and without
are the tools of creative co-existence and evolution.
May I learn to surrender to this process of becoming,
overcoming the fearsome kings,
pride, greed, carelessness, critical judgments,
that have reigned in the development of this I am that I am.

I am is brought to its knees,
in the humble acceptance of its failures at governance,
its sins of self-centeredness,
its ignorance of mystery and the divine.

Though I am is a product of the Great I AM,
His willful yes to Wisdom's loving embrace of humankind,
I am many times over a fool,
in search of what I cannot have,
wanting what I cannot possess,
yet all the while attempting to possess more
at the expense of others.
My lawless search for wisdom, knowledge, power
has lead to arrogance.
I am does not know the call of its own Creator.

Turn back I am,
see the radiant wisdom of your maker

found in the discipline of discipleship.
Rebel not against the boundaries,
limits that will one day lead to true freedom,
an inner kingdom of peace, integrity,
where one's definition of self is broad,
like the foundation of all selves
seeking footing in the turbulent waters of individuation.

May my tiny island that I am
become
what I AM intended me to be
when I was first imagined,
tiny yet somehow expansive
in its surrender, availability, potential.
May my yes to the He that reared me,
my understanding of She who nursed me,
lead me to freedom from the clutches of my enemies
within and without.

Let me courageously endeavor this fearsome tug of war
for dominance within the soul and body.
Let my journey along this mountainous edge
of personal development
forge a path to life's peak.

May I sustain,
in this trail into wilderness country,
a solid connection to those who go before,
follow,
though alone I must travel.
May my journey to servant-hood through discipleship
one day realize the vision I seek,
the I AM of us all.

Mother Divine

My heart and flesh
broken and tired
needing just a taste
of the flavors of my life.

Flavors from your kitchen-work in my soul,
a taste, the body's experience:
fullness, spice, sweetness,
a physical pleasure of connection.

What are you cooking up, my Dear?
All the chopping, grating, stirring
heating and transforming
simple things from my day
deep in my soul.

I long to know and share in
what You are doing,
where we are going
who I am becoming.
I long to co-operate in your efforts.

I need to smell, and see,
taste and chew
swallow and digest
the love you have for me.

Flaming Red Lit With Fire.
(a meditation before a red candle)
Valentine's Day, 2009

The color red,
the light that glistens from this candle,
whisper messages of hope.
Often I light candles when expecting friends into my home.
My hope is to reflect the warmth of sharing.

This flaming red candle has a gentle, quiet verbiage,
hope that goes beyond its light and warmth,
traveling faster, more passionately,
with its color and unspoken words.

Red reminds me of the menstrual cycle,
the monthly issue of blood,
shed by innumerable women,
for innumerable years,
all in anticipation of new life.

What about all the blood
shed during childbirth
for the sake of an infinite number of new lives?
All this blood lost,
wiped up with towels,
put into trash cans,
to serve seemingly no purpose,
like blood left on battlefields.

Where is our reverence
for this river of red,
feminine color of life
living things?

It is no small wonder to me,
when we celebrate Valentine's Day,
we do it with red,

efforts to be bold and heard.
For red is the color of blood,
in extreme cases,
sweat.

Blood, sweat, and tears.
I remember this red of passion and life,
in a man's single effort to give color and expression
to his last living event,
death as a hospice patient in 1984.
His bed clothes had to be changed every hour.
Shedding pink-tinged sweat from all the pores of his body,
he endured the labor and delivery of his second birth.

Will we survive this birthing process,
will our blood be spilled in vain and our prodigy die?

I hear of life,
humming of this color red,
its flame.
I have the power to blow it out
just as I had the power to ignite it.
I celebrate the color red,
its flow through my veins,
its flame in my heart.
Its quiet, passionate words
speak to me of the birth process
with all its promises
for life and fulfillment of dreams.

I will let red surround me.
I see it in flowers,
paintings,
sunsets,
my husband's hair.
I will remember my own mother,
her months of silent nourishing of me in the womb,
her labor for my birth.
I will not turn my back on my own daily issue of blood,

sweat, and tears
for the sake of life,
for the sake of my red life,
lit with fire.

Second Birthing
A meditation on Death and Dying

You are the Sun and Wind.
I am Rainbow.
I matter because I am a sign of the covenant
between Earth and Sky,
God and Man,
Spirit and Matter,
Sophia and Christ.
You are eternal,
I am moment,
like fire when the sun's rays are bent
through a prism onto the combustible.
I am a flash while you are forever Potential.

I will live but a moment.
Let me be transparent of the story,
the thread that is at the core of my life;
let me finish all that matters in my journey,
conception to eternal life.
Death and dying I know I must face,
like labor and delivery.
The shedding of what no longer fits,
dry bones rattling with life because of your breath,
the phoenix rising out of ashes.

What is this fear I feel at times all about?
Ashes,
shedding,
rattling
all make me quiver in my boots.
Bloody bones and scary eyes
part of my living and dying.

Grant that I not spend much time
in the darkness of the birth canal,
as I transition to eternal life.

Let my shedding of what no longer fits be quick,
my fears and restlessness be short lived,
as I open my senses to the unknown.
Help me walk into the light
that must be done through darkness
for the sake of my essence in you
which is pure, and true,
without blemish.

Let me leave behind matter that energizes others.
Be it my painting,
my creative writing,
my efforts to bandage the wounds of others.
Let something of what I have given my energy to,
be a source of life for humankind.
Let someone discover in the ashes of my living,
flecks of precious gold
to be saved and savored.

Joy in the performance of living,
rather than the recognition of its successes,
is what I hope to leave behind
in the dry bones and ashes of my existence.

There is a human hope for a pot of gold
at the end of the rainbow.
Rainbows show themselves in the most unique weather,
after storms,
through clouds,
on especially hot days
when rain is on its edge,
when sun and atmosphere unite in a most perfect manner.
May my life stand before others
as a sign that there is always reason to hope
in the midst of struggle,
that if not a pot of gold,
at least flecks of precious dreams and aspirations
can be discovered
by anyone who will search out its own end.

I am Rainbow,
I am matter,
I matter.
I am the result of Sun and Wind
bent though the prism of my existence
revealing hope and the intuitive fact:
life is worth the living and the dying.

Waves of Joy

Waves of joy
take me over.
This morning.
Rising, dawning,
awakening day.
Consciousness of You,
ground gained,
growing shoreline from
ocean's depths.

My soul and I
at one
with our togetherness.
Arms reaching wide around,
hugs from deep within
to all without.

Spasms of joy,
without explanation or logic.
Joy from tips of curled toes,
throughout,
grasping flesh,
grateful
anticipating,
eager for life,
to the fullness of a bowing head.

No reasoning but the reason
of a beating heart
feeling its own being
becoming.
Smiling soul
at one with its persona.
Tickling flesh
till laughter wells up

from deep within
the ocean of the belly.

Spasms of joy,
Moment's gift,
with no strings attached.
Union of body and soul
in a moment of fullness
for now,
moment in time.

Treasures

I pile the few treasures of my little space in this world,
patting them with pride and joy.
Failing to see beyond the gifts
with a gentle curtsey of gratitude to the Giver,
my joy and pride grow into greed and myopia,
filling me with emptiness and loneliness.

Penetrating Sun of Solitude.
I long,
endlessly it seems,
for your gaze to burn a hole in my pile of treasures,
into my heart,
so that I may follow the beam of light
to Your gaze,
discovering in a leap of faith,
groundless treasure,
Your life and energy.

Human greed and carelessness,
mediocre, ordinary,
the ground I walk on,
earth of me
eroded by wind, water, and time.
Enable this leap of faith,
courageously taken
across the canyon of my soul.

Holding fast
stones of my humanity,
treasures of my little world
with all their defects,
trusting in erosion and diminishment,
I find a lonely footing,
stepping into the mystery of Divine Presence.
Restlessness, apprehension, longing
transformed in the crucible of life,
lonely human search for love, acceptance, appreciation.

My pile of treasures with its pride and joy
becomes the stepping stone
causing me to stumble
falling, falling, falling.
Ultimately Your embrace.
The no-thing of You,
boundless, groundless treasure I seek the most,
hiding behind all that comes my way.

If only I will step into the things of my existence
with truth, self-reflection,
challenged to overcome fear.
Seeing the things I hold dear crumble into dust,
slip from my grasp,
leaving only me and my neediness.

Here in this moment of barrenness,
I find myself leaning on nothing.
No-thing fills me
with confidence, insight, compassion, creativity.

Your humble mystery,
hopeful-hiding in every moment,
dark reflection of who I am,
who I am called to become,
standing behind,
waiting, like a mirror.
True treasures found in companioning with You.

With fortitude, patience, mercy, and justice,
I say yes to my own search and rescue efforts,
self-discovery,
finding real treasure,
my soul,
given away in companionship,
the only real treasure I can possess.